IN A RELATIONSHIP...

Avoid the Worst and Experience the Best
in Your Social Life & Relationships

AARON BOE

© 2018 Aaron Boe. All Rights Reserved

All rights reserved. No part of this publication may be reproduced, distributed, or transmitted in any form or by any means, including photocopying, recording, or other electronic or mechanical methods, without the prior written permission of the publisher, except in the case of brief quotations embodied in critical reviews and certain other noncommercial uses permitted by copyright law. For permission requests, please contact the author at aaron@aaronboe.com

Interior book design by eBooks DesignWorks

Table of Contents

Introduction 15

The Story of The Woman Who Stopped Laughing 18

In a Relationship with Insight:
Uncommon Knowledge for the Journey 23

Five Ways to Increase Your Self-Confidence 25

Seven Strengths for Connecting 31

Seven Characteristics of a Healthy Relationship 39

In Love or Infatuation? 43

Healthy Physical Intimacy & Personal Standards 50

Five Key Concepts about Personal Boundaries & Consent . . 53

Two Essentials of Healthy Physical Intimacy 57

The Smartphone in a Healthy Relationship 60

How to Avoid Marrying the Wrong Person 74

Standards for Dealing with Disagreements 85

The Strength of Assertiveness 89

Warning Signs: Red Flag Attitudes & Behaviors 99

In a Relationship with Transitions:
The Breakup Strengths 111

The Strength of Moving On 112

It is Okay (or Better) to Be Single 121

Ending an Unhealthy or Abusive Relationship 124

When to Say Something to a Friend 130

In a Relationship with Reality:
The New Strategies for Social Safety 135

    Reality-Based Safety 137

    The Trust Principle 141

    Understanding Alcohol & Sexual Assault 146

    The Standard of Looking Out for Others 150

    Taking Action in Real-World Situations 163

In a Relationship with Friends:
Supporting a Friend Who Has Experienced Assault or Abuse   167

    Recognizing & Rising Above Victim-Blaming 169

    Understanding the Behaviors of a Victim/Survivor 170

    Things You Can Do to Support a Friend 172

References & Resources

    Online Resources 180

    Online References 182

    Books Referenced 183

    Recommended Books 185

    About the Author 189

For Mom, Dad, and Lisa.
For Lauren, Natalie, Jack, Maggie, and James. And for Kegan.
Because of you all, I know what love is and I know what matters.

And for my other sources of inspiration —
the young people of the world,
and the parents who love them.

From the Author

People often ask me, "How'd you get into that?" when they find out what I do.

Serving as a consultant on preventing sexual misconduct and abusive relationships sounds like an unusual career to many, but I also teach the other part, which is about healthy relationships, positive social lives and building healthy social cultures. I understand, though, why people cue in on the aspect of working on such serious social issues.

The answer to how I got into this type of work and why I wrote this book is not short, but it's quite simple.

One way to answer would be to say I know our social lives and relationships can be great—they can be full of fun, love, and connection with great people—but to experience those things we need to prevent and avoid the negative.

Another way to answer the question is I got into this work and I wrote this book because I wanted to.

I wanted to *do* something that could make a difference. I don't think I deserve any special credit for that; I'm just explaining that I felt compelled. I felt drawn to it, like I knew I could figure out how to do something to help.

To be more open, when I was a young man I learned that someone close to me—someone I really cared about—was hurt in one of the worst ways by a guy she knew and trusted, which is the most common way that type of harm occurs.

I didn't immediately start working on preventing that type of harm. I couldn't even talk about it. I did everything else. I put one foot in front of the other and kept going to school. I envisioned extreme violence for vengeance. I acted normal on the surface. I did a lot of things, but I didn't start working on the problem of regular people violating others and causing serious harm to them.

But I thought about it. I thought about it a lot.

The question of how an otherwise decent person could violate another person in one of the most harmful ways was on my mind every day, for what turned out to be decades.

If something burns within you for a couple decades, you can become pretty serious about figuring it out.

I do this work and wrote this book because I found some answers. I learned things that I believe every person, parent, and friend should know.

The issues covered in this book are complex, but there are insights and answers that are fairly easy to learn. I want everyone to have those answers.

I wrote this book for a lot of reasons, and here are some of them:

BECAUSE I have heard stories from parents—wonderful parents by any standards—sharing that they didn't see the signs that their daughter was in an abusive relationship until after real harm had occurred.

BECAUSE I know that at best, even healthy relationships can be complicated, and it can be difficult to discern between what is normal and what is not.

BECAUSE I obviously cannot reach and influence all boys and men who are capable of abusing or violating another person. Even if I could speak to an audience of men every day, and if our curriculum becomes implemented in thousands of organizations, schools, athletics departments, and part of campus education, we would only reach a small fraction of the men we should reach, so we must also equip girls and women to the best of our ability to avoid dangerous men.

I wrote this book because I know how boys and men are socialized, and how easy it can be for wrong behavior to seem normal to some of them.

BECAUSE I know how even a pretty good guy—I've tried pretty hard to be a good guy—can need additional education, and might still need to be challenged to be better.

BECAUSE I have seen the emotional trauma of a young woman who was violated by a person she knew and trusted. And because I understand the ripple effect throughout multiple areas of her life, lasting for years, and even decades in some ways.

It's not okay, and we need to prevent it.

I wrote this book because most people will at some point have a friend reveal that they have experienced abuse or sexual assault, and it matters how they respond when their friend shares that private reality.

BECAUSE even well-intentioned, smart people can say the wrong thing if they do not understand these confusing issues properly.

I wrote this book because preventing harm and avoiding bad relationships is better than figuring out how to respond *after* someone has already been violated and hurt.

I wrote this book because some of the most intelligent, confident, attractive women from great families tell me, "I was in an abusive relationship when I was younger."

BECAUSE I know people who have considered ending their lives because of the emotional trauma caused from being violated sexually, and because I have talked with a mom whose daughter did take her own life during the downward spiral of emotional trauma after rape.

BECAUSE a lot of sexual abuse happens *within* serious relationships, committed by a person claiming to care deeply about their partner.

I wrote this not only for women and girls, but also for men and boys because I have heard big, strong, confident men sharing about their relationships, not realizing their much smaller partner is being emotionally abusive in ways that should be unacceptable.

I wrote this book because conflict happens in all relationships, and it takes certain skills and standards to handle that conflict in healthy and productive ways.

> *I don't believe anyone should have to learn by trial and error in this central area of life.*

BECAUSE people who are capable of cruelty are often quite kind and caring at the beginning of a relationship. And many who would never commit physical violence might cause the most harm emotionally.

BECAUSE some of the most serious warning signs can be the most difficult to recognize.

BECAUSE relationships should be loving, caring, and the most fulfilling part of life. They should be free from fear and other toxic elements.

We must equip everyone to recognize when to avoid or leave a person who is either unable or unwilling to do their part of a healthy relationship, ideally *before* that person is able to cause serious harm.

BECAUSE many who will mistreat or abuse a partner sincerely believe they're not doing anything wrong—that their past behavior was justified under the circumstances—which means they haven't event considered changing. Others feel bad about past behavior, but their underlying attitudes will have them eventually acting in the same way.

I wanted to write this book because some people who mistreat and abuse partners come from difficult home lives, while others are from loving families. Some are from non-religious backgrounds, but others are strong Christians, or from another religious background. Some are under-educated, but others are highly educated. Some grew up in poverty, others grew up in homes with great wealth. Some are in small towns and rural areas, others in affluent suburbs, urban areas, and in every other kind of community.

They are in your community, and many of them are attractive, successful, and even friendly. Most of them are *not* mentally ill, and they have friends who will speak highly of them. That's a problem, and it's a problem we can't solve by just avoiding people who look scary.

I wanted to write a book that could put knowledge in your hands that could make a difference, either for you or for someone you love.

Sincerely,

Aaron Boe,
November 2017

Special Comments

This Book Applies to All People

The principles discussed in this book are applicable for any gender identification or sexuality. You will, at times, see gender pronouns of *he* and *she* used, or language used for an example that references a *woman* or a *guy*, rather than always using *they* or *the other person*. The principles, however, are the same for what is healthy and ethical and what is not, regardless of the gender of a person.

I write from my own experience and lens as a heterosexual male while trying to be inclusive and applicable to all readers. I sometimes use the word they in a sentence written about a singular person, which reinforces that the point is the same for any person. The singular use of the word they is an old practice in writing when referring to a person of unknown gender, or to a person whose gender is irrelevant, and is relatively common in speech. It is more common now to clearly communicate that the point is the same for any person.

This Book is Not Intended to Substitute Professional Assistance

The content in this publication is not intended to be a substitute for professional assistance. Anyone who has experienced a traumatic life event, which may include learning of a friend or loved one who has experienced a traumatic event, is encouraged to establish a relationship with a trained counselor, therapist, or psychiatrist.

Introduction

In a relationship...

Are you in a relationship?

Are you taking a break from being in a relationship?

Would you like to be in a relationship?

If you would like to be in a relationship, please allow me to correct you. What you really want is to be in a great relationship, or, at least in a healthy relationship that is loving, full of mutual respect, and is often great.

We receive little formal education about the challenges, skills, and responsibilities of each person in a relationship that is healthy.

Being intelligent and talented in other ways does not necessarily translate to knowing what it takes to be successful in a relationship.

Being in a relationship that is loving, caring, and full of consideration can dramatically improve the quality of your life.

If our friends, daughters, and sons can be in a relationship with a loving, caring, and considerate partner, it will improve the quality of their lives in countless ways.

In a relationship, conflict will happen at some point. Differences will reveal themselves, and disagreements will arise.

Being in a relationship with a person who is unwilling to rise above hurtful behaviors makes life very difficult, even if everything else is going well.

Even those who are in a great relationship can practice specific communication skills to make it even better.

You might have a friend who is in a relationship that concerns you.

You will know many people in your lifetime who have had very negative experiences from being in a relationship. It matters how we talk with a friend who has been in a bad or abusive relationship.

Some people want to take a break from being in a relationship, and that can be a good thing.

Before getting into a new relationship, there is a social life and a single life that requires advanced knowledge to avoid getting into a bad relationship.

All of us are in a relationship with many other people, and the principles of a successful romantic relationship are very similar to those that make relationships of any kind successful.

We can make our world a better place if each person has an elevated understanding of what it means to be in a relationship that is healthy, and the skills to make a healthy relationship even better.

The Story of The Woman Who Stopped Laughing

I have had the honor of working with several national women's organizations. In 2014, I was first approached by national staff from Zeta Tau Alpha Sorority and Sigma Nu Fraternity to discuss options for programs to prevent sexual assault. Those conversations and discussions with other organizations resulted in an initial group of a dozen organizations working toward change that would prevent sexual misconduct and abusive relationships while developing young people for healthy personal lives.

One organization I have enjoyed working with at the national level is Alpha Xi Delta Sorority. After providing them with an interactive workshop, materials, and training for their staff, I was asked to contribute an article for their national publication.

While happy to do so, initially I had no idea what to write. I thought for a while and decided to share a story of the time I met a hotel staff member who told me her friend had stopped laughing.

The story begins when I was checking into my hotel after speaking to a large group of students on relationships and preventing sexual assault. The woman at the desk was friendly and asked why I was in town. I often struggle to give a short answer to this common question because if I tell them I speak on preventing sexual assault and abusive relationships I assume people will think I just share statistics and tell awful stories. So even though people were waiting behind me to check in, once I gave the short version, I wanted to try to explain a little more.

I shared that I like to approach these serious issues from a more positive angle. I focus on healthy relationships and recognizing warning signs of unhealthy or abusive relationships because most abuse is not obvious physical violence, such as hitting.

As she pecked away at her computer, people were lining up behind me. I continued, "What a lot of people don't think about are signs like controlling behaviors, verbal cruelty, and emotional manipulation."

She looked up at me. She'd been listening the whole time. As she worked at getting my room key into its folder she said, "Yes, a lot of people don't realize that. Like, I have a friend who stopped laughing."

She had my attention. I had to hear her story. Her friend had stopped laughing?

Unconcerned that another person had joined the line behind me, she explained, "My friend had this distinctive laugh—really unique. And anytime she would laugh her boyfriend would make fun of her for it, in a critical way that made her feel self-conscious. It's like he was always implying that it was unattractive or made her sound dumb. He never hit her or was physically violent, but after a while, to avoid the criticism, she just stopped laughing."

As I often say, the label is not the point. We often don't need to debate whether or not a relationship should be labeled as "abusive" in order to acknowledge that it's not right. Would anyone want their sister, brother, or friend to be in a relationship in which they can't even laugh without fear of being criticized or belittled?

This example, of course, is just one illustration of how physical violence should not be the standard for determining a relationship is not good.

People tend to look for the wrong signs to determine if a relationship is unhealthy or abusive. They may say, "Well, I don't think he would ever hit her," or, "I don't think there's any physical violence going on," which can lessen concerns their friend is not in a healthy, respectful relationship.

In their own relationships, people can have strong positive feelings for a partner who treated them well at the beginning, and still might much of the time, so they tend to try to ignore a pattern of mistreatment such as cruel comments by comparing their relationship with something much worse, such as one that involves obvious physical violence.

Being belittled, demeaned, or controlled doesn't have to leave physical bruises to be wrong.

Having a standard among your circle of friends that each of you expects a basic level of respect, regardless of the situation, will embolden others around you and can make a life-changing difference.

In a Relationship with Insight

Uncommon Knowledge for the Journey

If you're going to be in a relationship, it is far better to have an advanced level of knowledge about this key area of life. Each of the following sections contains valuable insights in plain language, and each topic area can inspire you to seek more knowledge from the resources listed at the end of this book.

Five Ways to Increase Your Self-Confidence

Whether you are in a relationship or single, it is always a good time to grow as a person. Increasing self-confidence can result in multiple benefits both within and beyond relationships.

Most importantly, growing in self-confidence can make it easier to see the truth, that we deserve to be treated with respect in relationships of *all* kinds.

No one feels completely confident at all times and in all situations. We tend to think others are more confident than they are because most people don't openly share all of their insecurities, fears, and feelings of self-doubt.

Increasing your level of self-confidence can have a powerful effect on your life. Too many people assume they are stuck with their current level of confidence, as if it is fixed and cannot be improved. That is not the case at all. You can take control of most things in your life, and this is one of them.

Others assume they will naturally become more confident at some point in the future. That may be the case, but why wait? When a person becomes more confident as they grow older it is usually because they have learned to see themselves more as an equal to all others, or have simply let go of certain obstacles that held them back from greater confidence.

There is no reason to wait years or decades with the hope you will one day feel more confident. You have the power to increase your self-confidence now, and that can have a dramatic impact on your life throughout college and beyond. All it takes is the decision to do so.

1. **Do Things You Respect**
   Every time you make a choice to act in a way you respect, whether it's exercising, eating a healthy meal, studying when you'd rather do something else, or any other behavior that makes you feel good about yourself, it gives a little boost to your sense of self-respect. When you form the *habit* of doing something that builds your sense of self-respect, you create a consistent flow of positive energy toward your feelings of self-respect. This can have a profound effect on your self-confidence.

2. **Increase Your Knowledge**
   Knowledge builds confidence. Do what it takes to consistently increase your knowledge in a certain area, and you will notice your confidence increase in that area as well. There are answers available to almost any question you have on any topic.

When it comes to your knowledge regarding relationships and your social life, you will need to take ownership in educating yourself because in our culture it is not part of your formal education. You will gain insights by reading this book, and you can increase your knowledge even more by continuing to seek answers online, from other books, and from the wisdom of people around you whom you respect.

3. Accept Yourself & Move Forward

Feeling bad for doing something wrong can be healthy. It is part of learning to become the person you want to be. Too many people, however, assume they are supposed to keep carrying that guilt around, as if doing so makes them a better person. That is not the case.

Guilt can be useful to the extent that it helps you reflect on your actions, but after you have resolved to act differently next time, it is time to leave those feelings behind and move on. Reflect and resolve to do better next time and then let it go. You don't grow by carrying guilt; you grow by resolving to change and then implementing that change in your life.

4. Own More of Your Happiness

Own more of your happiness by not handing it over to others for them to determine how you should feel about yourself. For example, if you find yourself basing too much of your happiness on whether or not someone texts you back, take back ownership of your happiness.

We all like it when someone else is reciprocating interest, but your happiness should not all be in that other person's hands.

Your life is bigger than any one person's response to you, like returning a text. Your happiness is too important to put it all in someone else's hands.

5. **Have Substantive Standards**

   The typical person automatically puts an attractive person on a pedestal and makes that person out to be a trophy. Rather than committing this common error, it is more effective to have standards that go beneath the surface. People are like icebergs. Most of what makes up a person is beneath the surface and cannot be seen initially. It can increase your confidence to not immediately fall for what lies on the surface, as beautiful and attractive as it might be, because you refrain from automatically putting that person in a position of superiority to you.

   > *You reduce nervousness and intimidation if you refrain from putting others on a pedestal.*

   You are in a stronger position, and come across as more attractive, if you remind yourself that even though a person may be attractive, you do not know yet what it would be like to be with them. Remind yourself that a lot of people who are attractive would not be enjoyable to be with if they're not also going to meet other criteria, such as appreciating being with you and being a decent person in their behavior toward others. Substantive standards help you maintain a balanced perspective, which helps you make better decisions about with whom you should spend your time.

Courage Will Be Required

No matter how confident you become, there will be times when you do not feel confident and will need to practice the strength of courage to face your fears. Whether it involves making yourself talk to a person you find attractive, or hiding your fears and discomfort in a new social situation, it is important to know that it is completely normal to not always feel confident. Sometimes you have to move forward relying only on courage.

> *In order to optimize your social life,*
> *courage will be required.*

Courage is essential. If you always wait until you feel more confident, you will wait your life away, observing from the sidelines, annoyed with yourself for letting your fears run your life. Feeling confident is wonderful, but courage is even more important because it allows you to take action whether you feel confident or not. Move forward with courage, and confidence will catch up with you.

PERSONAL APPLICATION

One of the actions on How to Increase Your Self-Confidence that really stuck out to me was _____
_____
_____
_____

Two things I could focus on applying in my life are _____
_____
_____
_____

One thing I could begin doing tomorrow to move in this direction is _____
_____
_____
_____

Seven Strengths for Connecting

The ability to connect with others is a universal social skill, and it certainly doesn't hurt when it comes to talking with someone you find interesting. Even if you are in a fantastic, loving relationship, these seven strengths can apply to conversations in your work relationships, and just might help you help a friend with a bit of advice as well.

The following is a summary of the best I have learned from countless experiences of interacting with others, and analyzing (and over-analyzing) what worked and what didn't.

1. **Master the Other Part of Communication**
   Most people assume communication is about talking. The truth, however, is that communication is about listening as much as it is about expressing ideas and thoughts clearly.

   Aim to listen more than you talk in a conversation.

Spending more time listening than talking helps you in conversation because it requires you to practice being curious and inquisitive. When you utilize this social strength, you learn more about the other person. The result is that they feel respected and heard, which is critical for connecting.

2. **Get Your Focus Off of Yourself**
   Rather than worrying about being interesting, just be interested in the other person. This is the advice Jim Collins received from his mentor when he was a young professor at Stanford. Collins has gone on to write best-selling books for businesses and organizations, but he tells the story in *Good to Great and the Social Sectors* (2005) of how he first came to a powerful insight in terms of dealing with people.

   During my first year on the Stanford faculty in 1988, I sought out professor John Gardner for guidance on how I might become a better teacher. Gardner, former Secretary of Health, Education and Welfare, founder of Common Cause, and author of the classic text Self-Renewal, stung me with a comment that changed my life. "It occurs to me, Jim, that you spend too much time trying to be interesting," he said. "Why don't you invest more time in being interested?"

   When you are more concerned with the other person, you focus less on yourself. This helps you relax, and it increases your likability because people like others who are sincerely interested in them (and people are turned off by those who talk only about themselves).

Avoid the common error of trying too hard to impress the other person.

Trying to impress is quite unimpressive.

Share your thoughts or experiences only to the extent that it helps the conversation progress. It can be helpful to let the other person get to know a little bit about you, especially when it is to share something you have in common. But remember to be more interested in learning about the other person, rather than in trying to convince them how interesting you are.

3. **Find Anything in Common**
   Connection happens when you find something in common. The good news is it can be almost anything. We feel connected to people who have had a similar experience, and we love it when people agree with us.

4. **When You Don't Have Anything in Common**
   It doesn't have to be a problem if you discover, for example, that the other person has a different background and totally different interests. That just means there is a great opportunity to be sincerely interested—even fascinated—by the other person. It should make it easier to take the focus off yourself and be a curious, great listener.

Differences are opportunities for discussion.

5. **Make Connection Your Only Goal**
   It is easier to make a good impression and connect with a potential partner when that is your only goal. In other

words, set aside your desire to have this person fall for you. Get over your need for anything beyond a positive connection to happen. If possible, convince yourself that you don't even know if you would want it to lead to anything because you do not know yet if this person is the right one to spend time with.

A good salesperson, for example, needs to put aside his goal of selling something and just focus on making a personal connection with his customer. Of course he'd like to make a great sale, but in order to be highly effective he must make it his highest priority to just connect with the other person, independent of what it might lead to.

In fact, a salesperson can be most effective and most enjoy his job when he truly believes it doesn't matter if he makes a sale. Great salespeople cultivate a relationship with people, not only so it will increase the likelihood of business success, but because it is a better way to live.

When a salesperson is too focused on the sale, he turns people off, often costing himself the sale he wanted so badly. Salespeople appear shifty, shady or just selfish when they are too focused on the sale. Just as a salesperson needs to resist being overly concerned about making a sale, when you are approaching someone you find attractive it is important to let go of the need for it to lead to anything beyond a positive connection. Of course you'd like to have that option, but being overly concerned about it will decrease the odds of it happening.

> *It is harder to make a good first impression*
> *if you are trying to hide an agenda*
> *because an agenda is inherently selfish.*

Convince yourself that all you are doing is finding out if the other person is friendly and if you have something in common. Even if you think you want to be more than friends, you'll increase the likelihood of that happening if you're able to first just focus on making a new connection.

Even couples who have been together for years are wise to refocus just on connecting with the other person. The fact that people have spent years together does not mean they both feel emotionally connected and comfortable with each other. Too many agendas of trying to fix or control the other person can destroy that feeling of connectedness if they are not careful.

Connecting is about caring more about how the other person is doing than about what you want them to do for you.

> *People can feel it when you care how they are doing,*
> *and they can also feel it when you are*
> *more focused on yourself.*

6. **Be Different While Being Yourself**
   If you are meeting someone for the first time, it can be helpful to avoid approaching the conversation with the same topics everyone else uses. For example, if every other person asks the same two or three questions, you have a great opportunity to stand out with a little creativity.

In general, open ended questions can be better for conversation than questions that are just yes/no, or allow for one-word answers. An open-ended question requires a little more thought and is more likely to peak interest in the conversation for the other person.

For example, rather than asking someone you meet on a college campus, "So, what's your major?" you could ask questions like, "So, what do you think of your classes this semester?" or, "How have your professors been so far?" Others to try to include, "What do you think of it here?" or, "What do you want to do with your life?" It is important to communicate in ways that are comfortable for you, but these examples of more open-ended questions will invite more thought and better conversation.

Remember a conversation is not an interrogation—the other person is not on trial. Questions should be light and easy to answer, just not too generic. For example, unless there is a tornado coming, try to not be one of those people who attempts to relate by talking about the weather. Use the brain you've been given to get out of the mode of saying the most obvious thing, which is what most people do.

In addition to distinguishing yourself from the typical person by asking better questions in conversation, the other person might also feel more comfortable sharing more about themselves. This allows you to learn more about the other person, demonstrate your interest in listening more than you talk, and allow them to feel heard and understood. All of these things increase the likelihood of at least some kind of friendship or something more developing.

7. **No Need for Conflict**

   It is usually better to avoid sensitive topics, such as religion and politics, which are sensitive topics for many people. Even if you meet at a political organization, it is a better social skill to relate and connect on other topics. Additionally, get out of the habit of relying on labels to categorize yourself and everyone else. You are more than a label, and so are they.

PERSONAL APPLICATION

As I read this chapter, the strengths for connecting and staying connected that most resonated to me were _____
_____
_____
_____

The strengths for connecting and staying connected that I am going to immediately apply in my life are _____
_____
_____
_____

Seven Characteristics of a Healthy Relationship

Relationships can be complicated, but all healthy relationships have a number of things in common. Whether a couple has been together for years, or is just starting to spend time together, the principles are the same. Healthy relationships are characterized by certain ways in which two people treat each other and a number of positive things that are present within the relationship.

The following section does not contain a complete list of what is part of a healthy relationship, but it helps to paint a picture of what one looks like. Being clear on what a healthy relationship looks like equips you to recognize both positive signs and potential warning signs, so that you are better able to navigate your own personal relationships and be a supportive friend for others.

1. **Friendship**
    Each person likes who the other is as a whole person and respects many qualities and character traits in that person. Beyond feelings of physical attraction and love,

they have fun and enjoy spending time together aside from the physical aspect.

2. **Respect During Conflict**

   It is important to think about what a healthy relationship would look like even during challenging times. Differences and disagreements will eventually arise, even in the best relationships. In a healthy relationship, each person handles conflict in a productive way. Each person treats the other with at least a basic level of respect and consideration for their thoughts and feelings, even when they disagree or are angry with each other.

3. **Equal Rights**

   In a healthy relationship, each person treats the other as an equal. Even though two people are different, each person has the same basic rights in the relationship and as an individual with a life outside of the relationship. Neither person believes in controlling the other. When they have differences and disagreements, they discuss them. Each person has the same rights to share their opinions and to have wishes heard without being belittled or demeaned.

4. **Mutual Support**

   In a healthy relationship, couples support each other and encourage each other's pursuit of goals and healthy aspirations. Neither person works to limit the other from pursuing healthy activities or goals.

   It can be difficult, for example, to fully support a partner who wants to pursue a goal such as studying abroad or going to graduate school in another state, but healthy discussion of the challenges these endeavors might cause is important. A mature partner supports growth and openly addresses change in the relationship.

5. **Free of Fear**

   Neither person is afraid of the other, even during arguments or times of conflict. Beyond not engaging in acts that would evoke fear or intimidate, neither person would *want* the other to be fearful of physical harm or verbal cruelty.

6. **Healthy Independence**

   Neither person tries to control the other, and both have the right to express their feelings and be heard if they ever feel they are being controlled or manipulated by the other. Healthy independence is respected, and when one person questions the other's interest in activities outside the relationship, it is expressed openly and respectfully. Technology is used only to connect, not to control.

7. **Physical Intimacy is Healthy & Mutual**

   Both people have concern for the other's comfort, emotional enjoyment, and health in the physical aspect of the relationship. Both are above pressuring the other to engage in unwanted acts.

In summary, each person is confident in their own basic rights and the reality of those rights is respected by the other.

PERSONAL APPLICATION

It is important to think about what a healthy relationship looks like because _____
_____
_____
_____

The characteristic in this section that made me think the most was _____
_____
_____
_____

In Love or Infatuation?

Merriam Webster's definition of "infatuated" is:

1. To cause to be foolish: deprive of sound judgment
2. To inspire with a foolish or extravagant love or admiration

Infatuation is like a fake work of art that fools even the most skilled eye. If anything feels like love, it is infatuation. When we are infatuated with someone, we find it almost impossible to even consider that these feelings are not real love.

*Feelings are always "real,"
but it doesn't mean they are based in reality.*

Powerful feelings of attraction and admiration toward another person seem like they must be feelings of love. What else could real love feel like but this exciting feeling?

When we are infatuated with someone, it's like we have leaped over love and are in a state that obsessively focuses only on the positives of the person, many of which we are projecting on them, or assuming things about them that might not even be real.

I stumbled upon a great description of the term "crush" from author Alan Cohen. In his book, *Why Your Life Sucks and What You Can Do About It,* he explains that when we have a crush on someone, we are crushing the reality out of the person. We do not see them as the whole person they are with both strengths and weaknesses. We are unable to imagine or care about their weaknesses.

Something you thought was cute at the beginning of the relationship becomes extremely annoying after the infatuation has worn off and you see things more clearly. For example, when we are infatuated with someone, rather than seeing them as lazy and irresponsible we might see them as being "laid back."

Often when we are infatuated with someone we might even notice what should be an obvious warning sign, but we make an excuse for it.

Falling in love with an idea or a perception about a person rather than the real, whole person is not real love. It is thrilling, and those feelings may be for a person who is truly great, but it is not actually what love is.

If you realize you are seeing 100% positives in a person and then making excuses for anything that others would see as a problem, that's a pretty good sign you're closer to infatuation than being in love.

Starting in a state of infatuation might *lead* to a positive relationship. It could make perfect sense to stick around and see where the relationship goes because so far things seem good, but it takes time to really know a person and to see what it would be like to be in a relationship with them.

Love is Not At First Sight

Attraction is often at first sight, but attraction is not love. Love takes time, and "first sight" is obviously not a lot of time. Those who are happily together may say many years later it was love at first sight, but they are using a common saying to explain how it felt. Many who had horrible breakups would have also said at one point it was love at first sight. Immediate physical attraction and feeling of connection does not promise a positive, long-term (or even a positive short-term) relationship.

People say you cannot choose who you love, and they usually say that as an excuse for being in an unhealthy relationship. The truth is that you cannot choose to whom you are attracted, but attraction is not love.

> *Attraction is easy. Attraction is effortless.*
> *Attraction is involuntary.*

Love comes later. Love takes time, if it happens at all, and it is not something to work toward with every person we find attractive. Many people are physically attractive at first sight who would be an awful match as a partner.

As Dr. Jill Murray says, love is expressed in *behavior*. Another person demonstrates love for you in many ways, but it includes showing they are considerate of your feelings and what is important to you in your life. Another person showing you attention, or even affection for your body, does not mean they appreciate who you are as a person. Their behavior over time, not their words or flirtatious actions, will show if they respect and appreciate you.

Love is most real when it is for a person who doesn't just evoke feelings in your heart, but also your head. When we feel drawn to a person, and that attraction includes respecting them for their character and how their mind works, it's a safer bet that those are feelings of love that might also lead to a healthy relationship.

First sight can't figure out any of these things.

The "So Far" Technique

Here is a simple and powerful technique: instead of deciding right away the person you have fallen for is the ultimate match and you just *have to* make it work with them, learn these two words, "so far." The truth is you are interested in this person *so far.*

You do not know yet exactly what it would be like to be in a relationship with this person, or if you are already in a relationship you do not know what the future of the relationship would look like.

Even if it seems pretty good so far, the other person needs to continue to prove some things about who they are and how they would be in a relationship.

Have you ever been wrong before? If so, remind yourself that you have been wrong before about how great someone was going to be for you. Most of us have had the experience of being wrong about someone we were so certain about. Go ahead and jump in. But do not dive in heart first with your hands behind your back.

At the beginning of a relationship, if everything seems great, things are great *so far*.

Regain some balance and perspective after the initial off-balanced state of what people call "head over heels" in love with someone. When we put another person on a pedestal, we give them an unfair advantage they often don't deserve, and it doesn't necessarily help either person see what the relationship could be like. It puts more power back in your hands to still be attracted and interested, but cautiously optimistic based on the reality that you really, truly do not know what the future will hold.

It is good for the other person to feel they should keep proving themselves. It is good for them to see they don't get an easy pass because you think they're attractive. It is fair and right and reasonable for them to feel like they should see you as a whole person who deserves consideration for how you think and feel. They should be on their toes, and thinking of how they come across, rather than assuming they have already won and have the option to be in a relationship with you just because of their social status, looks, or any other surface level factor.

> *You are a person of infinite value and deserving of a person who treats you with care and consideration.*

If the other person does that so far, great. They should continue to do so if they want to prove they're worthy of your time and trust.

PERSONAL APPLICATION

The idea by Alan Cohen of thinking of a "crush" as a phase when we crush the reality out of a person could be helpful because _____
_____
_____
_____

Two reasons it could be smart and very helpful to regain balance and perspective at the beginning of a relationship are _____
_____
_____
_____

I could see the "So Far" Technique helping me, or helping me help a friend, because _____
_____
_____
_____

Healthy Physical Intimacy & Personal Standards

Healthy physical intimacy is not just about sex; it's about the entire spectrum of physical and sexual contact. This includes the personal space, boundaries, and basic rights of each person.

This section is not about judgment of an individual's personal choices, it's about what's healthy, and what kind of expectations a person should have for their partner's attitude and behaviors when it comes to personal space and each person's body.

Make Personal Standards Personal to You

What are your boundaries and your limits? How do you make decisions about what *you* are physically comfortable with in your social life and relationships? You might have noticed by this point in your life that you do not always agree with what others think your choices should be. However, have you truly taken ownership in making sure that your choices are completely your own?

As an adult, your personal standards and choices should be *personal to you.* That means they might not be the same as some of those around you, and that it is also not up to your partner to decide your standards. When it comes to anything that has to do with your body, it is up to you to decide what you feel 100% comfortable with happening.

The early physical and sexual experiences people have can range from loving, healthy and wonderful, to awkward, to very negative and even disturbing. Sometimes it is obvious that the way another person has acted was wrong, or even criminal. Other times, since early experiences with flirting, kissing and other physical interaction might have occurred with individuals who were very immature and acting in inappropriate ways (such as being selfish rather than having an equal concern for the other person's comfort) people can get the impression that these immature behaviors are normal. Unfortunately, some early partners are too immature and ignorant to act in healthy ways in a relationship, but we develop strong feelings for them anyway, and it can shape our thinking about what we should accept as normal in a relationship.

KEY CONCEPT
If a person was in an unhealthy relationship in the past, or is in one now, it should not be a source of shame. Shame doesn't help. Knowledge helps. Support from friends helps. Realizing that every person always deserves to be treated with basic respect helps.

When it is clear what healthy physical intimacy is, it becomes easier to expect that from any partner. Furthermore, it becomes easier to encourage all friends and others around you to feel emboldened to expect and demand appropriate respect as well.

About Consent, Boundaries & Ethics

A simple definition of consent:

> *An agreement to engage in a certain physical or sexual act that is freely expressed with either words or obvious actions, without any fear or threat, and at a time when one is capable of making that decision freely (meaning not incapacitated, such as from alcohol or another drug, sleeping, etc.).*

The word consent is often used in other parts of our culture to suggest a type of minimum acceptance of what will occur, such as signing a consent form for medical treatment, but that is not necessarily the meaning that consent should have in physical and sexual contact. Ethical and healthy physical intimacy is not about getting a person to relent, to give in, or to stop resisting. It is about both people freely choosing to engage in an act of their own free will.

Five Key Concepts about Personal Boundaries & Consent

1. **Most Basic Right**
   It is each person's most basic right that nothing should happen with her or his body that is not wanted at the time. Every person, regardless of who they are, their sexual history, or their social status has the inherent human right of bodily sovereignty, meaning they have the absolute right of control over their body.

2. **Moment to Moment**
   Each person has the right to change their mind at any time, and to have their decisions respected. Consent, or the agreement and desire to engage in a certain act, is moment to moment because a person's feelings and comfort level can change.

3. **Not Obligated**
   Agreeing to, engaging in or wanting one act is not necessarily agreeing to another. Just because a person

feels 100% comfortable engaging in one type of sexual contact, they should not feel obligated to engage in any other act they do not desire.

4. **Rights are Never Reduced**
   There is no point in a relationship when one partner has the right to engage in an act that is not wanted by the other at the time. If a couple has been together for a certain period of time it does not mean one person's most basic rights are reduced in any way. The principles of ethical behavior and consent are the same, even if a couple has had sex before or engaged in a sexual act before. Additionally, special events such as a dance or a birthday should not create automatic expectations or guarantees of sexual activity.

5. **Expect to Accept**
   It is completely appropriate for either person in any sexual situation to simply state, "I don't want to do that" or "No, I don't want to" or any other way of communicating that they do not want to do something, and to fully expect their partner to be 100% accepting of their wishes.

It is important to understand that although men are disproportionately responsible for acts of sexual violence and harassment, it is also possible for a woman to be responsible for both sexual harassment and sexual assault. If a woman neglects to confirm mutual desire for a certain act, she could be responsible for violating the most basic rights of a man or another woman. We must build a culture in which all people respect the same concepts of consent, boundaries and basic rights.

In her book *Coping with Date Rape and Acquaintance Rape*, Andrea Parrot tells the story of Eric, who was violated sexually by a woman, and experienced serious emotional harm from her actions. The story takes place during a study session.

> *Eric was nervous because he had never been very good with women, but he stayed anyway. After a while she started nuzzling up to him, which made him very uncomfortable, but he didn't know how to make her stop. He decided the best thing to do was to leave, but Maria began to fondle him and kiss him when he said he had to go. She asked, "What's the matter, don't you like me?" He said he did, but he had homework to do. He was very uncomfortable because he was a virgin. He didn't know what to do sexually, nor did he want to have sex with someone he didn't care about. Maria started to tease him and said there had been rumors in class that he was gay. If he didn't have sex with her she would know they were true.*
>
> *Eric was in a panic. He was afraid that if he left she would tell everyone he was gay. Then he would be rejected by his peers or perhaps beaten up. He was also embarrassed to tell Maria that he was a virgin. He had sex with her unwillingly and felt devastated afterwards. He felt used and dirty, but he did not know whom to talk to, or even what to say. (p. 107)*

In this story, Maria used coercion and neglected to confirm Eric was freely agreeing to sex when it finally occurred. It may be likely that she did not intend to cause emotional harm to Eric, but that is what occurred because of her actions. A person of any gender identification or sexuality can be responsible for violating another person sexually if they neglect to confirm mutual interest in that act.

When people practice two essentials of healthy physical intimacy, it ensures that if any sexual activity occurs it is a positive experience for them both.

Two Essentials of Healthy Physical Intimacy

Healthy physical intimacy includes mutual respect and a high level of concern about the other person's comfort level and enjoyment at all times. Any person who wants to be in your physical space and engage in any physical or sexual act, regardless of how long you have been in a relationship, should be on board with basic minimum standards of ethical and healthy physical intimacy.

Above Pressure of Any Kind
One basic standard is that each person refrains from pressuring the other to do anything physically or sexually that is not wanted at the time. Whining, begging, guilt trips and trying again and again to do something the other person is not 100% comfortable with is unhealthy and unethical.

It is completely appropriate to expect anyone who wants to be with you to be above pressure of any kind.

Having a Confirming Mentality

Healthy physical intimacy is not only pressure-free, but also includes the mentality of wanting to confirm the other person is comfortable with and enjoying that act at that time.

The most effective way to make certain the other person is 100% comfortable and wants to engage in that particular act, whether it's kissing or anything else, is by simply asking. For some people, this seems obvious, and for others, it seems unrealistic. They might wonder, "How are you supposed to ask, or how is my partner supposed to ask without it being awkward?" For a couple who has been together for a while, it might seem impractical or even silly to suggest that each should always ask the other if they want to do a certain thing, and then ask again, and then ask again for another act. But it is also true that no person should always assume they know exactly what the other person thinks or wants.

The larger point is about the mentality and the intentions of both people. If you ever feel like your partner (or a person you just met) is more focused on their own desires than they are on you and your mutual enjoyment and comfort, it is important to take that impression seriously. You are probably right. And, it is completely appropriate to fully expect anyone who wants to be with you to be as concerned about your comfort level, enjoyment, and excitement as they are about their own.

Whether it's kissing or any other sexual act, mutual enjoyment is a fundamental component of healthy physical intimacy. It is not a high standard to expect both people to confirm the other's comfort and enjoyment at all times—this should actually be a minimum expectation.

PERSONAL APPLICATION

It can be healthy to think through what I am comfortable with in terms of my own personal standards and expectations because _____
_____
_____
_____

The key concept(s) in the Five Key Concepts section that made me think the most was _____
_____
_____
_____

The Smartphone in a Healthy Relationship

Technology is covered throughout this book, but it felt right to have a chapter that specifically focuses on what smartphones and social media should be like in a healthy relationship, and ways of navigating the complicated world of technology in our social lives.

As with a lot of things, how situations play out in real life can seem complicated, but the principles are quite simple. The way a person should act in person is the same as how they should act online. The principles of basic respect—the responsibility to consider the other's feelings and rise above cruel, threatening, or controlling behaviors—regardless of the situation, are the same. These responsibilities are not removed or reduced simply because a phone is between two people.

The App is Not the Issue
A new app or social media platform can come out next month or next year, but the principles of what is healthy and ethical, and what is not, remain the same.

What remains the same is the responsibility to act in ways that show consideration and care, and to rise above wrong and hurtful behaviors. We are responsible for our actions toward others, and we must always consider the effects our actions can have on others. This is never truer than for those with whom we are in a close personal relationship.

Just as positive words of flirting, care, or compliments in a text have their meaning, negative or mean words have powerful meaning as well. A partner in a healthy relationship does not use the power of their smartphone to:

- Mess with their partner's head
- Manipulate
- Threaten
- Harass, or follow when the other wants space
- Make them feel demeaned or less than
- Belittle
- Coerce them into sending pics their partner doesn't want to send
- Demand their partner stay awake to text when it's late and their partner wants to sleep for school or work
- Share private photos, or hold private photos or texts against them to blackmail or coerce
- Share screen shots of private conversations in order to be cruel
- Say things they wouldn't or shouldn't say in person

Do those behaviors sound like love?

Of course not, which is why the principles of how a person should act with technology are the same for how they should act in person. Those behaviors are not loving, caring, or considerate. Texting, sending photos, and posting comments are behaviors—they are choices, and better choices are always available.

In a healthy relationship, each person is responsible for choosing behaviors that express care, consideration, and build up their partners with love. Even when relationships are difficult, such as during times of conflict, responsible partners rise above cruelty, threats, extreme selfishness, demands to invade or violate privacy, and anything else that does not honor the other's feelings.

Healthy Independence Online

One characteristic of healthy relationships is Healthy Independence. This means that not only should a person feel like they can be supported in pursuing their favorite personal interests, but they should also feel they have some healthy independence online. As I discuss in Warning Signs, jealousy can be a very natural human feeling, but it does not remove a person's responsibility to act right.

As I have written in other sections, technology should be used to connect, not to control.

Even if a person is struggling with feelings of jealousy or possessiveness, those are feelings they need to deal with *without* thinking it justifies controlling their partner or demanding access to all private spaces. And a person's phone and accounts that require a password are certainly private spaces.

Feelings Can Be Good Clues

My friend Dr. Brian Mistler, who is a brilliant psychologist, said something years ago that stuck with me. He said, "The feeling itself can be a warning sign." It struck me as profound, and I felt a little foolish that I'd forgotten this important truth. I had been so focused on learning about what is "out there" to recognize and analyze, I was overlooking one of the most relevant indicators of something being wrong.

When we start to analyze our own relationship or the relationship of someone we care about, we tend to want to look outside for complicated clues and discern between what is and isn't a big deal. We tend to look at the other person's behavior. The instinct to do that is correct, and we need to continually evaluate, especially if we're concerned with unacceptable or dangerous behavior, but a lot of times one of the most powerful indicators is already within us, or already within the person we care about. If someone *feels* scared of their partner, for example, that is enough of an indicator that something is seriously wrong. (Does making another person scared of you sound loving?)

If you *feel* negative feelings, pay attention to that. If you feel hurt—if you frequently feel emotional pain in response to your partner's words or actions, take those feelings seriously. Sometimes we possibly overreact and have negative feelings we shouldn't blame on another person, but much of the time our feelings are powerful indicators of something wrong.

In a healthy relationship, each person is able to share feelings if something is bothering them. If something feels wrong and you want to bring it up in a respectful way (*see the section on The Strength of Assertiveness*), it is your partner's responsibility to listen and consider your feelings. And it is your partner's responsibility to respect reasonable wishes and requests for how you feel your relationship could be healthier. For example, if it *feels* like your privacy is being invaded, then maybe it is. You don't even have to ask, "Is this normal?" because you can feel in your gut that you'd like to have more privacy.

Just as you should feel like you can have a private conversation with someone over the phone without it being listened to or recorded for your partner to review, you should feel you can have a private conversation via text without your partner reading that conversation.

The Power of Personal Rules

One technique that can help you avoid saying things you may regret or adding fuel to a fire is to have a set of Personal Rules for your phone. They're called personal rules because you are choosing them for yourself. It is you who believes in them as smart guides for your actions, and it is you who accepts that it would be wise to not break them.

One example of a personal rule someone might choose for themselves is to not look at their phone after a certain time of night. The rule could include charging it in another room or shutting it off completely after a set time. Many executives and highly accomplished professionals do this because it helps them lead a more peaceful life, rather than responding non-stop to emails or other messages over the course of their week.

One of the simplest personal rules is, "I don't have that app on my phone" or "I'm not even on that app. I don't use that at all." It might feel like you *have to* be on certain social media platforms, but it's worth considering... Do you really? Would the quality of your life maybe be *better* if you weren't constantly checking a certain one? If your life could be *better*, then it's not a wild idea to consider cutting an app out entirely.

A different example of a personal rule could have to do with negative feelings. For example, a smart personal rule could be, "Not when jealous. I won't text or post when I'm feeling bothered by feelings of jealousy, or if I'm feeling possessive. I choose to rise above it and focus on something else."

When we are especially bothered by difficult emotions, they cloud our thinking and we are more likely to say something foolish or come across in a way we may later regret. Additionally, acting impulsively can feed our negative feelings and keep us from working on moving beyond them.

"I don't text out of anger." That's a personal rule I use.

Have you ever said the wrong thing when you're angry? I have. At some point we do need to communicate with our partners, but when one or both people are very angry they might need to first take a minute to make sure they're able to talk assertively, with self-control, rather than aggressively (see section on The Strength of Assertiveness).

When you are communicating online or over text and feel you cannot have a productive conversation because you are too upset or angry, it is much more effective to end the conversation for the moment and explain that you need to calm down a little before you can have a productive conversation. And if your partner is acting in unacceptable ways online, it is always appropriate to say you are not going to communicate until they can talk to you without being cruel or acting in that way.

A personal rule of, "I don't text out of anger" or "I only text or comment when I'm certain I have self-control" can be helpful for our social and professional lives in general.

I remember seeing an exchange of comments from a person who is an author, has a PhD, and is highly respected in many circles. He was arguing about an issue with another person and resorted to making threatening comments. He acted like a child, and I now have little respect for him even though up until then I'd heard people speak very highly of him.

It is important for our relationships, and our lives in general, to have a system of personal rules that keeps us from acting in ways online or over texts that can backfire, ruin relationships, or lead to a lack of respect from others.

"Normal" is Not a Good Standard

When we perceive that many of our friends or peers act a certain way, it can be difficult to maintain our own standards when they are different. When a certain behavior is accepted as "normal," we tend to think that means it's fine, or even the right way to handle things.

Asking yourself what is normal for how to handle yourself with your smartphone or online is a foolish way to choose how you should act. A lot of behaviors are common, but they are unhealthy, they don't gain the respect of others, and they can ruin relationships.

Most people have not thought through what they're doing, why they're doing it, and what the consequences could be. Even highly intelligent people, or people who are good friends overall, might handle their communication online unwisely.

So, don't look around you to see what's normal. Think about what is respectful, practices self-control, and is a way of operating you can feel proud of. We don't build a great life for ourselves by just looking around us and doing whatever other people do.

See sections on *Warning Signs: Red Flag Behaviors and Attitudes*, *Seven Characteristics of Healthy Relationships*, and other sections in this book that help paint a clearer picture of what's normal and what's not, and how smartphones, social media, and technology are tools that can help a healthy relationship, or that can make an unhealthy or abusive relationship much worse.

He's Not Going to Delete It

What advice would you give to a younger person you care about regarding social media and smartphones? Specifically, what advice would you give them regarding what kind of pictures they should or should not send to another person?

This simple exercise is very good to think through because we tend to give better advice to others than we follow ourselves. Thinking through the smartest ways to deal with social media and smartphones empowers you to prepare yourself in advance for how to best handle certain challenges.

You might say to a younger person, "Do not send a photo of yourself to another person unless you plan on sending it to the rest of the world as well."

You might say, "Screen shots! Taking a picture of the picture with another phone! It's stored somewhere in the cloud! Whatever! But stop assuming a picture really goes away and exists nowhere."

You might say to a friend or younger person, "No matter what the other person promises, they're not going to delete it. And they're probably going to share it with someone else."

There is one fact we can all agree on, and it's that once you press "send" it is out of your control forever.

You Don't Need To

Sending private pics you wouldn't want others to see is somewhat risky with even the most trustworthy person, and an extremely high risk with most people. The larger point is this: it's not necessary.

If a person is interested in you, they will continue to be interested without receiving an explicit photo of you. For example, women have been attracting and exciting guys throughout all of human history without sending pictures of their naked or partly-naked bodies. If a guy tells you he *needs* a photo, he is being manipulative. He *wants* it, sure, but he doesn't need it and you don't need to send it to prove anything about yourself.

The Future is Unknown

Even if you can trust another person one day, it does not mean you can trust that they will be considerate of your privacy forever. Roughly half of *marriages* don't even last forever, and photos are permanent. They last a long, long time.

A lot of guys who are decent people for the most part don't think it's wrong to share photos with buddies that were not meant to be shown to anyone else. Just like an exciting story, it can almost feel like he *has to* share it with at least someone.

You may want to believe a person if they tell you they will delete a photo right after you send it, or that they won't take a screen shot of it. That's possible, of course. It's wise, however, to consider the likelihood that they won't delete it and will have access to that photo forever.

Manipulation Means "No"

If a person knows they may be sending a photo that will be shared with the entire world, that is one thing, but if they are pressured into sending something they're not comfortable with, that is extremely selfish and wrong.

Emotional manipulation should be an immediate wake up call. If someone is attempting to be manipulative, refuse to go along with whatever the person is trying to get you to do. You shouldn't feel pressured to do anything with your body, including anything that has to do with an image of it that will be out of your control forever.

How might someone try to pressure you?

"C'mon, don't you trust me?" **(No.)**

"Everybody sends pics. Especially for their boyfriend/girlfriend." **(Not everybody. And other people are not me).**

Or, he may take the reverse psychology approach.

"I bet you won't do this. You're too scared. You won't do it. You're not that fun." **(You're right, I won't. I don't need to.)**

If it doesn't feel 100% right or comfortable for you, then you can view that feeling as your head and heart telling you that you don't need to do it, or that it's not a good idea even if you think you'd like to do something. If the other person cares about you more than their own self-interests, they wouldn't want you to do anything you're not 100% comfortable with.

Any hint of manipulation should be a reminder to resist and to question his level of real respect for you.

Anything You Send Can and May Be Used Against You

How difficult would it be to share your private photo with every one of their friends? Whether it is after a fight or after a break up, if the impulse would strike this person they would have what could be a very powerful card to hold against you. One of the most pathetic things any person can do is to use a sensitive photo as leverage to threaten you, but a partner or an ex may be tempted to do that very thing.

A controlling or vindictive person might say, "You'll do what I want you to do or everyone will see the photo you sent me." That is manipulative and wrong, but it is also a realistic possibility. A wise person remembers that all bad break ups are of relationships that were just fine at one point.

You Have an Excuse

Calmly stating a personal standard such as, "I don't send photos like that of me," ideally will shut down requests for them. However, if you feel you need a supporting reason, let them know that while it may be true they would never share it with anyone, it's possible a friend would someday grab their phone and find the photo. Who knows what another person would then do with it?

There might be other creative reasons for refusing to send private photos of yourself, but you shouldn't need extra reasons. You should expect a partner to not want you to do anything that you don't feel completely comfortable with and think is a good thing to do.

PERSONAL APPLICATION

Two things I have seen some people consider as normal ways of interacting with others using their smartphone that I believe should not be are _____

_____
_____
_____

Two Personal Rules I could apply in my life that could make a difference are _____

_____
_____
_____

A person should not feel pressured to send any kind of pic they're not completely comfortable with sending because

_____
_____
_____

How to Avoid Marrying the Wrong Person

Feelings of love can lead to thoughts of marriage.

For something as serious as a lifelong commitment, and one that will impact every aspect of your life, it makes sense to think pretty seriously about it. And thinking seriously about it means getting beyond the excitement of thinking you have found "the one" or planning a fun wedding.

It calls for the work of self-awareness and the discipline of being honest with yourself.

Let's get something out of the way. I don't know who should and shouldn't be married, and it's none of my business what other people choose to do. With that acknowledgement out of the way, I believe there are some observations worth sharing.

A Healthy Fear
When we feel cautious and concerned because there is a lot at stake in moving a relationship toward engagement and

marriage, we have a healthy fear. It is wise to have a healthy fear of marriage.

A person could have an *unhealthy* fear of marriage, which could be expressed by assuming they would absolutely never want to even consider getting married and refusing to enter into even a committed relationship with another person they really care about. I do *not* want anyone to have an unhealthy fear of marriage. But a healthy fear can be valuable because it means a person comprehends the seriousness of the situation.

There is no ceremony, vow, or special event that can magically make a relationship better than it is. It can be fun to dream about a beautiful wedding and envision how great life will be with a certain person, but the reality is it is the most serious and important decision a person can make.

Even Long Movies are Short

I watch a lot of movies. I'm not picky. If it appears to have a good story, I'll give it a try. And being a guy doesn't mean I don't like a good love story or romantic comedy.

I have a saying, however, that "movies only last an hour and a half." The point is, a good romantic comedy or love story often ends on a high note. The couple gets together for a happy ending, often resulting in a cool wedding and some music that makes us feel great.

That's what movies are supposed to do. They're supposed to take us on an emotional journey with a happy ending.

The implication, of course, is that all is well now, and it will be from now on, but is that realistic? Sometimes I think it would be interesting to have a sequel showing the couple's arguments, the differences they have to work through, and the very real conflicts that occur between people who are two different human beings with different personalities, challenges, and goals.

None of us is born with a great marriage guarantee. Countless intelligent and loving people have ended up in unhealthy or abusive marriages.

The most effective way to avoid an unhealthy or bad marriage is to avoid marrying the wrong person, or at least the wrong person for you. It also helps to avoid getting married for the wrong reasons.

How Not to Choose

How do you avoid marrying the wrong person for you? One powerful way is to avoid being *in a relationship* with a person who is not right for you.

It can sometimes be difficult to discern this right away, so the next best thing is to have the courage to leave a relationship with a person once it does become apparent this is not the right match for you. Sometimes even a good-hearted person with great qualities is nice to be in a relationship with, but that doesn't necessarily mean marriage is the next best step.

It's hard to say who *should* get married. The section on *Seven Characteristics of Healthy Relationships* offers some strong things to consider. But it can also be very helpful to at least avoid some of the bad reasons people choose to marry someone.

A Dozen Bad Reasons to Get Married

1. **They think it is the next thing to do in life after college, and the person they're with seems to be alright.**

   This is what you could call "the next phase" assumption. Choosing to marry a person with whom you're in a healthy relationship isn't wrong, but deciding to do so just because you assume "it's time" isn't a good enough reason for two people to commit their lives to each other.

2. **They believe this person is the right one because he is different from the last guy who turned out to be the wrong one.**

   It may be that you made an error in judgment in the past and do not want to end up with a person who has the same issues as your ex, but that does not mean being *different* from what annoyed you before qualifies this person for a lifelong partnership.

3. **They get caught up in how happy they think it would make their parents to see them married to this person.**

   Your mom is not marrying this person. A wise woman, for example, knows that her mom might be very excited about her daughter getting married, but that she only *should* be excited if it is going to be to the right person for her daughter.

It might be true that more people should probably listen to their parents more often and consider the wisdom they have acquired in their lifetime, but the idea of your parents being excited for you, or wanting you to be with a person they assume is a great catch should not be a primary motivation for a life-long decision. Make sure you don't put the feelings of others over your own, and certainly don't allow those feelings to distract from other concerns you may have.

4. **They become a wedding planner.**
   They get caught up in how exciting it would be to have the wedding they're envisioning. They get excited about the music, the flowers, the bridesmaids, and the family attending. This exciting vision can cloud their thinking, and is a real problem if there are serious issues to consider.

   My grandmother used to say, "The bigger the wedding, the shorter the marriage." This saying has probably not been verified by research, but her point was that some people spend too much time fantasizing about and planning a wedding and not enough time seriously contemplating the marriage partnership to ensure they know what they are getting into. Weddings are beautiful celebrations of a couple's love. They can create a ceremony around the life-long commitment being made. Planning a party can be great fun, but it is truly a fantasy to believe a gorgeous wedding guarantees a good marriage, or that it can fix serious problems within a relationship.

5. They do it because the other person wants to.

He bought her a ring, he proposed, therefore she has to go through with it, right? No. That's incorrect. A sweet marriage proposal does not set in motion things that cannot be reversed.

If a guy is going to propose, which is the traditional way (but people can be non-traditional), it is nice if he puts some thought into making it a special event. It is more important, however, that the right thought is put into things *before* the decision to buy a ring. We men can be foolish with our feelings and make very poor choices, as you have probably observed, so a proposal should not mean an engagement and marriage must follow it.

I think of it as "The McDonald's Test." A guy should not propose at a McDonald's, but he should only propose after they have sat at a McDonald's and other places that are not especially romantic or special, and had sober discussions about real issues in life and marriage.

6. They talk themselves into it.

It is one thing to enter into a marriage knowing some challenges will arise at some point. It is a different thing to have to work at ignoring real concerns or denying issues that, when you're honest with yourself, seem like problems with the relationship.

Sometimes these problems might not even be with the other person and are instead based in one's own feelings. For example, a person might be in a relationship with a great partner, but not feel like she wants to marry that person. Other times, the issues are most certainly with the other person's character and past behaviors. A person shouldn't have to do a lot of work to talk themselves into "looking on the bright side."

7. They let the fear of ending up alone override their concerns.

Some people do not make this error but instead reject every decent person who does not fit into a set of extremely specific surface-level standards, which may include some combination of looks, wealth, and personality. They approach dating and relationships as if they couldn't possibly ever end up alone.

The other extreme is the larger problem, which is choosing to marry a person they don't feel right about because they worry about ending up alone, or fear getting "too old" and not being married with a family. The point is, each of us must work to be honest with ourselves if we have real concerns about the other person or about a relationship, even if certain desires like wanting to be married and have a family are strong.

8. They tell themselves they won't find anyone better.

If a person has serious concerns about their partner's character, or the relationship, or feels mistreated in any way, they should not get married to that person, at least not as long as those serious concerns remain.

Some concerns about a partner are fairly minor. For example, if someone wants their partner to dress better, having a conversation about that might be easy enough. If, however, they need to become a *better person*, that is not as easy to fix as shopping for new clothes. Hoping serious issues or concerns about a person's moral character, work ethic, ways they handle themselves when they're angry, addictions, or any other aspect of their personality will improve is not a safe bet.

Each human being who is in a romantic relationship with another person deserves for the relationship to be caring and for it to be free from certain negatives, such as abuse or fear of it. There is a difference between a person maturing enough to stop looking for a fairy tale prince and seeing the value in the regular, great human being in front of them, and ignoring major concerns about a partner. No one should ignore real problems by telling themselves they won't find anyone better.

9. **They think that once they are married he will grow up and change his ways.**
Do not expect a person to change for the better after the wedding. (And don't expect that *you* will magically change for the better because of a wedding).

Yes, many people tend to mature as they grow older, but you do not want the job of trying to make a person grow up. It can take decades or a lifetime for a person to change, and certain aspects of their personality will never change.

Change can be hard even if a person *wants* to change, and many people who act in selfish ways don't really want to change. They want to find a person who will let them keep getting away with being how they are.

10. They don't soberly and seriously consider the phrase, "For better or for worse."

That's a pretty serious vow. For better, *or for worse*?

To make an unconditional commitment is very different than a commitment based on the condition that things will be as good, or better, than they are now. People can get sick. Accidents can happen, resulting in life-altering changes. People can lose jobs and struggle financially. Most people are pretty decent at their best, but not everyone has the character to be the partner you would want to be attached to during difficult times.

11. They don't consider that a life partner is a partner in every sense of the word, and most of it has nothing to do with being a sexual partner.

There is no sex life that can make up for the gaps in an unhealthy relationship long-term. Choosing a partner for marriage is like choosing a partner for business, for traveling, for living together, for sharing money, for sharing responsibility, and most likely, for sharing parenting. It is sharing every aspect of your life with this *one* other person for as long as you live.

12. They try to ignore or deny past abusive behaviors.

Don't marry — or stay with — a partner who has been abusive, either physically or verbally. And threats and intimidation (making you scared) are abuses of power. See the section on Warning Signs: Red Flags Attitudes and Behaviors. Do not ignore a pattern of behavior or attitudes that fall into categories listed in Warning Signs. Wishful thinking will not solve serious problems.

A person who can be abusive or mistreat their partner in any way while in a dating relationship will often increase their feelings of ownership and increase their manipulative or domineering behaviors once they have the more formal, legal relationship of a marriage. They might believe marriage entitles them to certain special privileges or an imbalance of power, or they might just realize it would be even harder for their partner to get out of the relationship since it would require divorce.

Why think about marriage if you're single?

Why would it be helpful to think about marriage before you're anywhere near it? Because if a person seems to not have the character of a person you'd want to marry and have a family with, and if a person does not treat you in a way that shows the proper care and respect each person deserves from a life-partner, this can be a big clue it might not be worth investing much of your time and feelings into that person and a relationship with them.

It's harder to meet the right person if you're in a relationship with the wrong one. It's harder to end up in a relationship with a person who treats you with respect and appreciates you if you spend all your time with a person who doesn't appreciate and respect you.

PERSONAL APPLICATION

A "healthy fear" of marriage, rather than an unhealthy fear, would simply mean _____

_____

_____

_____

Two of the Dozen Bad Reasons to Get Married that stuck out to me were _____

_____

_____

_____

It would be wise for a person to think seriously about what it would take for a healthy marriage, even when they are still single or just dating because _____

_____

_____

_____

Standards for Dealing with Disagreements

Maintaining Composure and Expecting it in Return

No one is always at their best, but their worst needs to be not that bad.

> *Composure: a calmness especially of mind, manner, or appearance*

When two people are in a relationship long enough, they will eventually disagree. It is normal and inevitable that there will be differences of opinion, different life goals, and different wants.

> *Conflict itself is not the problem;*
> *it is how each person deals with it that matters.*

Just as feelings of jealousy and insecurity do not excuse controlling or manipulative behaviors, feelings of anger do not justify cruel or abusive behaviors.

Restraint: *control over your behavior*

The way we handle ourselves when arguing or disagreeing with a partner can mean the difference between resolving the conflict and making things much worse. It can mean the difference between respecting ourselves for how we handled it and feeling ashamed of ourselves. It can also mean the difference between maintaining a great relationship and losing that person.

All people get angry, but only some think that means it's okay to physically or verbally mistreat their partner.

Anger is Not a Viable Excuse

Everyone gets angry; most people choose not to express anger with cruelty because they have concrete minimum standards for being above that behavior. The following quote is from Lundy Bancroft, who spent fifteen years working with abusive men.

"When a new client says to me, 'I'm in your program because of my anger,' I respond, 'No, you're not, you're here because of your *abuse*. Everybody gets angry. But they don't necessarily abuse their partners.'"

It's not about poor communication or a lack of conflict resolution skills. As Bancroft puts it in his book *Why Does He Do That?,* most abusers have normal abilities in conflict resolution, self-control and communication when they choose to use them. They typically get through tense situations at work or in other areas of life without threatening anyone. An abusive person is not *unable* to resolve conflict non-abusively; they are *unwilling* to do so with their partner in a relationship. An abusive act is a *choice*, because a different choice was always an option.

Alcohol is Not a Viable Excuse

Part of how we know partner abuse is not caused by substances is that many alcoholics and drug addicts are not mean to or controlling of their partners. For example, the abuse of alcohol among men on college campuses is a very real problem, but because most men who drink to excess do not violate others sexually or abuse their partners, alcohol and other drugs are not the core issue, and should not be used as an excuse for a person's behavior.

Alcohol does not remove or reduce your responsibility for anything you say or do in your interactions with others. Intoxication does not ever work as a defense for a person's behaviors. A person might receive sympathy or forgiveness from some of their friends, but ultimately, each person is responsible for all of their actions.

To even attempt to excuse one's behavior by pointing toward alcohol use only adds to the case against a person's character and does nothing to reduce their culpability. A man, for example, who mistreats or violates another person, and then seeks to minimize his responsibility or defend himself by pointing to his drinking and intoxication, is a man who has shown he is responsible for failure to act with basic decency, failure to maintain self-control *and* failure to take responsibility for his actions.

Provocation is Not a Viable Excuse

Sometimes people attempt to defend the wrong actions of one person by focusing on the other party's actions. People might say, "Well, she deserved it for acting that way." It is important to understand that even if a partner's actions are wrong and would make anyone angry, it does not remove the responsibility to respond in a non-abusive way.

Provocation is not the point. It is quite possible that one person would provoke a strong reaction from the other, but an abusive response is still unacceptable.

It's natural to want to respond strongly when we are angry, but a truly strong response is to be *above* any kind of abuse. A truly strong response to inappropriate behavior is to maintain composure, express what is wrong about the other person's behavior, and state that you will not spend time with a person who treats you like that.

When you practice restraint, and maintain composure in the face of another's negative behavior—when you "take the high road," as the saying goes—you leave the other person to face their own wrongdoing, rather than giving them an opportunity to point toward your poor behavior as well.

The Strength of Assertiveness

Assertiveness is often confused with aggressiveness, but they are not the same. Learning to be more assertive is not about learning to push others around to get your way. It's about saying what you want to say, but doing so in a self-controlled and respectable way.

Most people have a tendency to either lean toward being a little too cautious about saying what they want to say, or a little too quick to speak without pausing to consider the other person's perspective. The trick is to find the right balance in communicating, which is usually somewhere in the middle. Finding the proper middle way, which we call assertiveness, benefits both you and the other person in any kind of relationship.

Domineering: *tending too often to tell people what to do; often trying to control the behavior of others*

There are reasons why being too aggressive does not work for a relationship, or for one's self. Even if you get your way short-term by being forceful, it builds resentment in the other person. If you express what bothers you without self-control, you put the other person in a defensive position and at the very least, you are more likely to make a fool of yourself.

However, constantly and passively giving in to the wishes of your partner can have a cost as well. When you do not speak up about what bothers you, it can chip away at your self-respect, and it does not advance the relationship forward in the way that open communication does.

Passive: *accepting what other people do or decide without trying to change anything, even when you feel you should*

The Middle Way

Assertiveness could be called the middle way. It's the option in between the two extremes. And even though finding the perfect balance can take some skill, just being aware of the concept and looking for the middle way can have very powerful results. To get a feel for what assertiveness is, consider the following list of examples:

Assertiveness is the middle way—

> **Between** being a pushover, and being dominant.

> **Between** being superior, and being inferior or subordinate.

> **Between** being silent, and being violent.

Between not saying what is bothering you, and yelling about what is bothering you.

Between never sharing when you see things differently, and frequently being argumentative.

Between neglecting your own rights, and neglecting the other person's rights.

Between not honoring your own feelings, and not considering the other person's feelings.

Assertiveness is about —

Having both self-respect and showing respect for the other person.

Each person being able to say what they need to say, but doing so in a way that is considerate of the other person's feelings as well.

Three Key Benefits of Assertiveness

1. **The other person is more likely to hear what you're saying.** When you are aggressive, the other person might be too defensive to consider what it is you are saying. When you are too passive, and do not even say what you are thinking or feeling, then it is unreasonable to assume the other person can guess what you are thinking or feeling. It is always fair for both people to share what their feelings are, and it is always a minimum standard that each remains above threats, intimidation, cruelty, or manipulation.

2. **It builds self-respect and your sense of self-worth.**

   When you honor your own impulses to say something, and do so in a composed way, you behave in a way that is respectable, which feeds your sense of self-respect. The experience of speaking up, especially if it took some courage to do so, reinforces the fact that your thoughts are worthy of being heard. You deserve to say what is on your mind. Realizing this feeds a positive cycle that helps to build self-respect and self-worth, which helps you feel more confident in the notion that you deserve to be treated with respect.

3. **Other people respect it.**

   People do not respect aggressiveness. They might fear it, but they do not respect it. Being domineering is not the proper alternative to being a pushover. Some people make the error of assuming those are the only two options, so to avoid one extreme they go to the other extreme. The middle way is more effective, and it is what people respect.

Applying Assertiveness during Conflict

The solution for dealing with anger in a healthy way is to express how you feel, but in a self-controlled way that rises above abusive behaviors. At times of intense anger it might be necessary for one or both partners to walk away or remain silent because they do not feel able to express themselves effectively yet. Ultimately, however, communicating effectively is the key to resolving conflict. And, assertive communication is almost always the most effective type of communication.

Some people make foolish statements if their aggressive behavior is challenged. They say things like, "What am I supposed to do, be a pushover and let people walk all over me?" They make this type of dismissive statement as if the only two options are pushing others around or being a pushover. Are those the only two ways people can interact with each other in a relationship? Of course they're not. There is always an alternative that involves both self-respect and self-control. The strongest option is saying what one wants to say, but doing so with composure and restraint, and basic consideration for the other person.

Assertiveness & Listening

> "Seek first to understand, then to be understood. This principle is the key to effective interpersonal communication."
>
> —Stephen Covey

In many cases, the most effective way to communicate is to *not* try to express your perspective first. Being assertive is not only about how you speak, it is about how you communicate, and effective communication involves effective *listening*.

To paraphrase Covey in his classic book *The 7 Habits of Highly Effective People*, in order to interact effectively with your partner, your child, your coworker, your friend—you first need to understand their perspective. Listening is powerful because it gives you accurate information to work with. Instead of assuming you already know what the other person is thinking (or neglecting to care), if you listen first you're able to have a much more productive conversation. You can't maximize communication unless you have an accurate understanding of where the other person is coming from.

The assertive mentality is about self-respect *and* respect for the other person, so being assertive can simply mean bringing up a topic or issue that you feel needs to be discussed. Sometimes it means exercising the courage to start a much-needed conversation. When an assertive man wonders what is going on in his relationship, he respectfully addresses it. And the most effective way to address an issue with another person is to first try to understand their point of view.

Listen first—it's more effective.

People who act aggressively, instead of assertively, miss out on gaining the insight of how their partner sees the situation, and they increase the odds of looking foolish when they misunderstand the other person's perspective. On the other hand, people who are too passive experience anxiety and stress because they wonder what is going on, but do not muster the courage to ask questions. Address the issue, first by trying to understand the other person, and then maintain composure as you share your perspective.

How to Express Yourself Assertively during Times of Conflict

The classic I-statement formula can be a very effective way to communicate. Robert Bolton, Ph.D. covers I-statements well in his book *People Skills*. His simple process involves pointing out the other person's specific *behavior* (rather than a personal attack), and then explaining how what they have said or done has made you feel and affected you.

The I-Statement Formula

"When you _____,

I feel _____."

Example 1: When you look down at your phone when I'm trying to tell you a story, I feel like you're not listening to me and that you don't care.

Example 2: When you talk about your ex, even in a negative way, I feel like you're still thinking about your ex and it bothers me.

Example Phrases that Open Conversations to Share Perspectives

"Tell me what's going on, please."

"Is there something we should talk about?"

"Help me understand how you see things."

"I know we need to talk about _____. Tell me what you're thinking."

"What did I do that you think was not right? Tell me what I did that upset you."

"Is there something bothering you that we should talk about?"

"I feel pretty angry about things right now, but I want to first understand things from your perspective. Tell me what you're thinking."

Additional Examples of Assertive Communication

"I don't necessarily agree with that."

"We need to talk about this. I don't think we are understanding each other."

"I want to understand your perspective, but don't yell at me."

"I still do not feel heard."

"Calm down, please, if you're going to tell me what you want to say."

"I don't feel respected right now."

Sometimes a person might experience a very high level of anger, but that does not give permission to use threats or verbal cruelty. In their book, *Your Perfect Right*, Alberti and Emmons provide example statements that allow a person to express anger without lowering themselves to verbal cruelty or threats:

Expressing Anger

"I'm very angry right now."

"I strongly disagree with you."

"I get so mad when you say that."

"I'm very disturbed by this whole thing."

"It's not okay to talk to me like that."

"That's not fair."

"I really do not like that."

"I'm mad, and I'm not going to put up with this anymore."

Notice that Alberti's and Emmons' statements express how a person feels without name-calling, personal attacks, guilt trips or threats. They do, however, clearly express frustration or anger, and that something needs to be talked about.

As long as you do so with self-control, it is not only appropriate to express your anger verbally, it actually *helps* the other person understand what upsets you. When both people in a relationship try to move toward a solution, that practice can strengthen their relationship.

Treat everyone well, and expect the same in return. In doing so, you will live in a way that attracts people and earns their respect.

PERSONAL APPLICATION

The benefits I see of listening first are _____

_____

_____

_____

Self-control and assertiveness is better than aggressive language because _____

_____

_____

_____

Some of the ways I could practice being more assertive are ___

_____

_____

_____

The benefits I can see in being more assertive—using "the middle way" of communication—include _____

_____

_____

_____

I will rise above being either too aggressive or too passive in the following areas of my life _____

_____

_____

_____

Warning Signs: Red Flag Attitudes & Behaviors

"When someone shows you who they are, believe them the first time."

—Maya Angelou

When you are able to recognize the attitudes and actions that could be signs of trouble ahead, you increase the odds of avoiding someone who might be toxic in your own life, and you are better able to help a friend as well.

Ownership Attitudes

In our culture we often use language such as, "This is *my* boyfriend. This is *my* girlfriend." Or, "This is *my* partner." It is natural for people to feel some level of possessiveness, or a strong desire to keep that person as a partner and not see them end up with anyone else. Some people, however, have an ownership attitude that is more literal, and this attitude can lead them to engage in some unhealthy or abusive behaviors.

No one says at the very beginning of a relationship that they will tell their partner what she can and cannot do, nor do they come right out and admit they will manipulate her to gain more control, but some reveal their attitude in their language. Comments like, "I would never allow my girlfriend to do that" or "I would let my wife do that if she wanted to, as long as our kids were in school" are warning signs of a controlling mentality. The key words here are "allow" and "let" because they imply that the person saying them is in control and has the right to say what does or does not happen. Some people will use the word "obey," which clearly suggests authority over the other.

Mistreating or Speaking Harshly about Others

Most people are very careful how they act toward a potential partner when they first meet, but they might reveal things about themselves by how they treat or talk about others. For example, if a guy is polite to you but is demeaning to a server at a restaurant, or cruel to a younger guy on his team or in his fraternity, that is an expression of his maturity level and character. If a guy speaks in demeaning ways about other women, such as referring to a woman as a "slut" or other derogatory term, that is a red flag.

Controlling Behaviors

Each partner should rise above attempts to control the other. One of the top things to expect any partner to be above is the act of telling you what you can and cannot do.

Most people who try to control their partner do so in ways that are not as obvious as explicitly telling their partner what they can and cannot do. Instead, they use emotional manipulation, such as guilt trips, pouting, or the silent treatment. They might belittle and demean their partner to reduce their self-worth so they are easier to control. Some will start a fight or will resort to a guilt trip any time their partner considers doing anything they don't want them to do.

Controlling behaviors are often not violent at first, and they may be exhibited by a person who would never be physically violent, but if they limit your freedom in unnecessary ways, then they are wrong and not part of a healthy relationship.

Isolating Behaviors

It can seem like a sign of strong interest for a partner to "want to have you all to himself." It could feel flattering for a person to only want you to be with them. There is a difference, however, between having a strong interest in being with you and having a strong interest in *controlling* you and keeping you from your other relationships.

If you do not feel totally comfortable with your level of freedom and your ability to do what is important to you beyond the relationship, it is important to recognize that and talk about it with your partner. A partner who respects you and is committed to a healthy relationship will take your feelings seriously, and will respect reasonable requests for changes.

Wanting to spend time with family and friends is a normal, healthy thing. Anything that is good and healthy for you should be accepted, respected, and encouraged by your partner, even if your partner would miss you when you're not there.

Invasion of Privacy

Just as you have physical boundaries that should never be violated, you also have a basic right to privacy as well. A partner should not demand open access to your personal items. Going through messages on your phone, looking through your personal things, such as your backpack, purse, or drawers in your room, is an intrusion that is not part of a relationship in which healthy space is provided.

You should not feel obligated to share your passwords to your e-mail, phone, social media accounts, or any other personal space having to do with technology. If it feels like a violation of your privacy, then it probably is. Jealousy and insecurity are common feelings, but those feelings do not mean a person can deal with them by disregarding the other person's basic boundaries.

Verbal Cruelty

Some people who would never use physical violence will feel totally fine saying things that are unacceptable. Too often, people excuse their behavior by labeling it as "normal," or by contrasting it with more extreme abusive behaviors to make it seem less wrong. But just because saying cruel words, such as name-calling, is not the same as hitting or shoving, that does not make it right or acceptable.

In addition to the fact that verbal abuse is wrong and hurtful, it is important to recognize how serious it is because sometimes verbal abuse precedes physical abuse. Even if verbal cruelty would not precede physical violence, verbal cruelty is not okay. No person is justified in demeaning, belittling, or criticizing another in ways that can be personally hurtful.

Verbal cruelty is not part of a loving relationship. You deserve to be with a person who treats you with respect at all times, so verbal cruelty can be a clear sign to move on.
For more see the section on Ending an Unhealthy or Abusive Relationship.

Emotional Abuse

It could be said that all types of abuse are emotional abuse because any kind of threat or violation is felt emotionally. Physical abuse certainly has an emotional impact. However, emotional abuse is most commonly defined as using your emotions against you, such as playing mind games or using your feelings to manipulate and control you. Emotional abuse can be far more serious than just saying something hurtful. As the authors of *When Dating Becomes Dangerous* say, "Emotional abuse also causes wounds such as self-doubt, self-hatred, shame, feelings of going crazy, or feeling unable to survive without the abuser."

Examples of emotional abuse include verbal cruelty in the form of comments suggesting no one else would want you, and then pointing to a supposed imperfection as the reasons for that, or playing on insecurities and being critical about your body. Sending mixed signals that mess with a person's mind, such as saying something mean while professing love at the same time is also an example of emotional abuse. Criticizing appearance, calling a person fat or constantly suggesting they are crazy are all hurtful and unacceptable ways of treating a partner.

Using Technology to Control, Limit, or Abuse

In a healthy relationship, smart phones can be fantastic tools to stay connected and increase intimacy. In an unhealthy or abusive relationship, however, technology is often used to monitor, track, and control what the other person does.

> A smartphone should be used to connect, not to control.

Technology should not be used as a tool to restrict or limit the other person's basic freedoms. Verbal and emotional abuse can also be done through technology. A partner in a healthy relationship will never use technology in a way that makes you feel controlled or mistreated in any way.

The potential for technology to be used for retaliation or blackmail is very high, and it should be taken seriously. It would be wrong for a person to post or share a private picture or video their partner wouldn't want shared. With the potential for negative consequences, it may be wise to remove the possibility by not providing a partner with digital photos you wouldn't want others to see. Everyone should strongly consider the digital photos they take, especially if they may be of a compromising nature. Recognize that pressure to do anything in which you are not 100% comfortable is not right.

Pressure to take and send a picture or video of a sexual nature might seem somewhat common, but that doesn't mean it is okay. Just as no one should be pressured, coerced, or threatened into doing anything sexually she does not feel comfortable doing, no one should be pressured to take and send sexual pictures or videos, even on an app such as Snapchat, where the messages "disappear."

Threats

Physical force is obviously an example of very serious and abusive behavior, but so is the *threat* of any force. Like most of the behaviors we are discussing, use of threats is not a warning sign of an abusive relationship, it is *already* abusive.

For example, even if a woman cannot picture her partner ever hitting her, any threat, intimidation, or implication that physical harm is even a possibility expresses behavior that is wrong, and reveals a way of thinking that is dangerous.

When to Seek Guidance

The preceding examples are not a complete list of abusive behaviors or warning signs. If you are concerned about your relationship or that of a sister, brother, or friend, talk with a professional in person, online, or both, for guidance on what steps to take next.

As soon as you start to question a partner's behavior, or as soon as you start to become concerned about the relationship of someone you know, it is important to seek guidance from resources online and on campus. You do not have to know all of the answers, and you do not have to handle everything on your own. You might, however, need to be the one who starts the process of learning more about what to do next.

The Label is Not the Point

Some behaviors might not seem like something that should be called "abusive," but they are unfair and they could be a sign of an underlying mentality that is not conducive to a healthy, great relationship. If you ever find yourself debating about whether or not a certain behavior would be considered abusive, that is at least a warning sign something is wrong.

If it is unacceptable and wrong behavior, it does not always matter what it is labeled. Most people who are in an unhealthy relationship know something is not right. It does not feel like a happy relationship, despite the fact that there are some good times. And most will, at least sometimes, think to themselves that certain ways of being treated were wrong.

In a healthy relationship, people might have different opinions and different wants, but those differences would result in a discussion about how they might come to an agreeable solution.

In an unhealthy relationship, one person would take control and make decisions without giving the wants and wishes of the other equal value.

In an abusive relationship, one person makes demands and uses physical, verbal, emotional or other types of mistreatment to get what they want.

Examples of Unhealthy & Abusive Behaviors

Emotional Abuse & Manipulation

- Threatening a breakup to manipulate & get one's way
- Accusing partner of being "too sensitive" after being cruel
- Playing on insecurities and saying their partner "can't take a joke"
- Threatening suicide or self-harm
- Using silence as a mind game

Verbal Abuse

- Name-calling
- Cruelty, meanness
- Belittling
- Demeaning
- Embarrassing their partner on purpose in front of others

Physical *(Threats, Intimidation & Force)*

- Threats of physical harm
- Destroying personal property
- Preventing a partner from leaving a room by blocking the door
- Pushing or shoving
- Physical force of any kind, even if it's not slapping or hitting
- Squeezing arm, towering over, or any actions used for intimidation

Examples of Unhealthy & Abusive Behaviors *(continued)*

Technology

- Demanding access/passwords to accounts
- Monitoring and tracking where their partner is and controlling who they can and can't be with
- Pressuring to take & send sexual photos

Isolating Behavior

- Keeping partner from healthy relationships with family and friends
- Insisting that their partner end friendships

Physical *(Sexual)*

- Insensitive to partner's comfort level & feelings about engaging in a certain act
- Pressure to engage in a sexual act
- Attitudes & behaviors other than absolute concern for partner's enjoyment & mutual respect of physical intimacy

PERSONAL APPLICATION

The Red Flag Behavior that stuck out to me most was ____

_____

_____

_____

Technology is often misused in relationships by _____

_____

_____

_____

The things I want to be more conscious of looking out for in my own or a friend's relationship are _____

_____

_____

_____

In a Relationship with Transitions

The Breakup Strengths

The Strength of Moving On

It can take strength to move on after a relationship has ended, just like it can take strength to break an addiction. Moving on after a breakup is like re-discovering how to live without a key person in your life. It is completely natural for it to be a challenge.

Any breakup can be difficult. I believe it's fair to say the sting is much sharper when someone breaks up with you, but it can also be difficult and painful even when it is your idea to end a relationship.

You are not alone if you experience another person breaking up with you. You are part of a very large club! It's a club full of members who didn't want to be part of it, and often don't know how to talk about it.

Countless others have felt dejected and hurt after a breakup, and no one likes the way it feels. Few people talk about the hurt openly, but everyone who goes through it feels a similar pain. We are in this together. We have survived, and you will too.

Understanding the Pain

A breakup can make you feel like not only is your heart broken, but your life is too. In your relationship you and your partner had a routine of activities and you were experiencing very positive feelings, but now the source of that has been removed. You may have had expectations of a certain future with that person, complete with pictures in your mind of how great it would be. Those have been shattered. It is a disorienting feeling to have a significant part of your life change in an instant, particularly if the choice was not yours.

The first step is to decide to move on.

Focusing on getting this person back obviously is not deciding to move on, and will stall your ability to heal emotionally.

Trying to get back *at* a person who broke up with you is not the right thing to do either. Saying cruel things online, texting hateful messages to try to hurt the other person, or any other kind of "getting back at" your ex are often overreactions that are not fair and things you'd likely be ashamed of eventually. Rise above it. Retaliation is not an expression of any kind of strength.

Deciding you are going to make your ex jealous will not help you move on.

Waiting until your ex sees they made a mistake and begs to have you back, just guarantees a certain level of misery, and will not help you move on.

The above attitudes still focus most of your energy on the other person. Your valuable energy, which needs to be spent moving on, is being given to your ex in those behaviors. I understand that tendency, but I do not recommend it.

Resolve to rise above the need to have that person's affection. Declare your freedom—declare your independence from needing that person for your happiness. You may have to fight a war with yourself to gain your emotional independence, but you must first decide it is what you want and deserve.

It's Not About Your Ex

Your life is too short to spend it being concerned with the wrong person for you. You do not need to believe the other person is horrible (although sometimes it helps), but you do need to decide it is time for you to figure out how you are going to live a fantastic life beyond a relationship that is now in the past.

The person who has caused us pain is a common character in the videos of our minds.

It can be difficult to reduce the number of appearances a person makes in your thoughts, but it is essential to decide you will do just that.

You are more than any person's desire to be or not be with you, and you are more than anything that happens to you.

Move On by Moving Your Focus

Direct your attention toward yourself, not to wallow in sadness, but so you can grow beyond the need to be with your ex. Make your goal to grow beyond the need to depend on *any* one person for your happiness.

Avoid focusing directly on replacing this other person. Doing so still orients your decisions around your ex and continues a feeling of neediness for another person. Your goal must be to become whole again, independent of another person's affection.

In order to move on, you need to shift your focus away from the other person and toward things that make you feel stronger and better about yourself.

Move On by Moving Yourself

When we feel pain, we want to do something to reduce it. Some choices, of course, are smarter than others. Some of the common ways of trying to cope with difficult emotions are not very healthy, such as using alcohol, food, or engaging in risky behavior, and can be dangerous.

Rather than looking for ways to numb pain, make a decision to get better than ever. Don't get better to make your ex jealous. You're moving on. You're focusing forward. Decide to get better than ever as a gift for *yourself.*

We can use pain to propel us forward. We need to do something with all of that negative energy, so making a gut-level, serious commitment to move toward exciting goals can be the best choice following a breakup.

Taylor Swift has used the pain of breakups to make new music that her fans love. Not all of us can turn hurt feelings into millions of dollars in our bank account, but it's a good example of putting negative energy into creative energy. She has moved forward rather than let it tear her down.

One of the more effective ways to help shift the focus back to yourself is to focus on your complete health, meaning your body, mind and spirit. Since a breakup can be painful, you need an exciting and healthy goal to distract you from it and give you something to feel good about again.

You move on more quickly by *moving* yourself. Take action. Move your body and your mind. Run, walk, workout, do yoga. Do all of it.

Feed your body and your mind with good things, and you will grow beyond your current state and regain proper perspective. Read good books about good things. If you want to read a great book about getting over a breakup, I recommend Lisa Steadman's book, *It's a Breakup Not a Breakdown.*

Taking care of yourself and moving toward big goals will help you see there is a happier, healthier life for you beyond the relationship that is now in the past.

Apply your negative internal energy to positive actions and you will respond to this challenging experience by growing stronger than ever.

Spend time with good friends. It reminds you that you are lovable and deserving of people who appreciate you. You are deserving of care, respect, and appreciation.

Don't Underestimate the Value of Being Free

Eventually, part of moving on is beginning a new relationship. This may seem like a daunting exercise or an exciting opportunity. It may be both.

The person who is not right for you (and they're not, because the relationship ended) is no longer holding you back from moving on to a better life and finding the person who *is* right for you. It might not be the very next person you meet, but being free from a relationship that wasn't completely right is a very good thing.

When You Still See Each Other

Processing the end of a relationship can be especially complicated when emotional attachments and physical attraction linger on. This can happen regardless of who decided to end the relationship.

When strong feelings remain, it can be incredibly tempting to try to keep the door open on the relationship. It can be easy to convince ourselves that it makes perfect sense to meet up with or even continue a physical relationship with an ex. Unfortunately, it just isn't so simple. Doing so typically causes more damage, and it delays the healing process.

Participating in a flimsier version of a relationship can result in a roller coaster of emotions that make the breakup process even more painful. It delays the healing process and eliminates most or all progress made. It reopens wounds and hurts. And, typically, it allows one person to take advantage of the other's feelings.

Don't forget one person is less interested in being together as a couple than the other; otherwise you would remain together in a fully committed relationship. The person less interested in a relationship but still interested in "hanging out" or "talking" is usually gaining the advantage of having their ego fed and perhaps a physical relationship without providing their partner with the security and devotion of a commitment. That's a pretty good deal, for one person only!

Maybe in Another Lifetime

You cannot begin to move on until you cut off communications.

You may think, "Can't we still be friends?"

Yes, you can be friends in another lifetime. That different lifetime might come within a few years or a few months, but it is not now. It qualifies as another lifetime when both of you have fully moved on *and* when both of you can handle the idea of just being friends. Be prepared for those conditions to never be met. It may never happen.

It is essential for both people to see the relationship that ended as something of the past. In other words, regardless of what the future might bring, that particular relationship is done.

You may think, "Isn't it possible to start over and make it work this time?"

It may be possible in another lifetime. It is *possible*, it just can't happen until a real break has taken place and there is some distance between your relationship and the two of you. Don't plan on trying to make it work right away and expect it to be automatically healthier than it was.

Time to heal means time away from your ex.

After you have grown beyond the relationship and come to peace with everything, it may be possible to have a very cool relationship with your ex as friends. That would be wonderful, but it's not common. When we try it too soon, it very rarely works and usually causes excess pain.

Giving It Another Try
Sometimes ex partners decide they want to get back together. Before you do this, ask yourself some questions. Are you certain you want to do this, not just because you feel lonely? Are you certain your decision is not motivated by a desire to prevent the other person from moving on? Are you certain you're not just trying to prove something to yourself?

If you are both choosing to get back together, maybe it is for the best. Who knows? There is, however, a smart way to go about it.

If you are going to get back together with an ex, don't try to start right where you left off, especially with the physical part of your relationship. Start over and go slowly. To the extent that it is possible, start the relationship from the beginning in every way. Build a healthy relationship from the ground up. Reconnect emotionally without using physical intimacy to do so. A person who really wants to get back together should want to be with you independent of the physical relationship, and your relationship can only work if it is built upon a great deal more than the physical.

If both you and your ex are excited about getting back together, consider re-reading this section and taking a minute to think. Consider talking with friends you care about, and who you know care about you, not just the friend who will tell you what you want to hear.

If two people are equally committed to creating a new, positive relationship, then it's possible they could have a great relationship. But that is only true if *both* are serious about doing what it takes for a relationship to be healthy. It is easy for an ex to say words or show attention that expresses interest. If someone breaks up with you, it should not be an easy thing for them to have your full attention and commitment again.

There are exceptions to rules sometimes, but a general principle of life is that new and better things await when we move on and move forward.

It is Okay (or Better) to Be Single

It's harder to meet the right person if you spend all your time with the wrong one.

Everyone knows someone who has always been in a serious relationship. If one ended they were quickly into another one. That is not necessarily a bad thing, but neither is being single.

Some people just like being in a relationship, and they might coincidentally meet a great person right after a relationship ended. But others have an unhealthy motivation to be in a relationship at all times.

It can be very healthy to spend time on your own. Developing your own interests, spending time with friends and family, and even volunteering enriches you and your overall life experience.

It is better to be in a healthy relationship with yourself than an unhealthy relationship with another person.

It is also much better to be single, working on strengthening yourself, than to be in a relationship with a person who is not treating you with proper care and concern. Never stay in a relationship with a person who is verbally or emotionally manipulative or cruel.

It is always a good time to focus on taking proper care of yourself and ensuring you feel good about yourself and the direction you are heading. Whether you are experiencing the difficult period immediately after a bad breakup, or you haven't been in a relationship in a while or ever, spending time on cultivating other aspects of your life can be very enriching. You might find out something about yourself that was important to learn.

Do You Really Need a Relationship?
If we are not careful, many of us have a tendency to become a bit needy or desperate when we are single. When we feel needy, we are not in the best state of mind to meet someone new. When we are off balance, we are not in a stable position—we are not in a position of strength. When we are in this "needy" state of mind, we are more likely to ignore flaws that might be important to see. It can also be easier for someone else to take advantage of us because it is more difficult to stick to our personal standards of the kind of character we want in a person.

Be especially careful of dating or looking for a new relationship when you recognize through self-awareness that you are feeling desperate or especially needy. Consider talking with a professional and working on strengthening your feelings of self-worth and self-confidence.

It can be very natural to *want* a relationship, and more people who want a healthy relationship should exercise the courage to pursue one. But beware of thinking you *need* to be in a relationship.

When You Stop Looking You Might Find Someone

Here's a piece of wisdom that rhymes: Spend most of your energy on you, but be open to meeting someone new. Not everything that rhymes or sounds good is true, but there is something to the notion of just focusing on being happy with yourself while single and working to set and achieve personal goals.

We can be open to something, without having too much concern about it. Remember, you don't want "a relationship," you want a healthy, positive relationship.

It is a somewhat common experience for a person to finally give up looking and then very quickly meet someone. Often this happens because confidence is more attractive than neediness.

Focusing on yourself and your personal growth and development (not just physically, but mentally and spiritually) is a gift to yourself, and it also happens to be very effective in attracting people to your life. When you have grown as a person while outside of a relationship, you are in a better position to be able to have a successful relationship when you meet the right person.

Work on finding happiness within yourself and by yourself. And be open to finding the right person who is able to see and appreciate the many things that are great about you.

Ending an Unhealthy or Abusive Relationship

Ending any relationship can be stressful, but getting out of a relationship in which the other person has behaved in troubling ways can be even more complicated. The first thing to remember is this simple truth: You have a basic right to leave any relationship.

> *You are not obligated to make accommodations for a person who has mistreated you.*

The following tips and suggestions can be good food for thought, even for ending a relationship that is *not abusive* or especially unhealthy.

When ending any relationship, but especially an unhealthy relationship, it is helpful to be emotionally prepared for the following:

- Promises to change
- Apologies
- Tears
- Signs of sincere remorsefulness

- Threats of self-harm
- Guilt trips
- Anger
- Criticism and claims that you will never find anyone better, or anyone who cares about you like he/she does
- Refusal to accept the break up
- Attempts to get you to feel sorry for him/her
- Working through your friends or family to pressure you to get back together

CAUTION:

Helping a friend get out of a relationship that is violent, or could be violent, should include talking with a professional. Talk with a counselor or call a hotline. Go to loveisrespect.org and chat online with a professional. Get professional advice somewhere on how to get out of an abusive or potentially violent relationship safely.

The following considerations were inspired by the work of Patti Occhiuzzo Giggans and Barrie Levy in *When Dating Becomes Dangerous*:

> It may seem cruel to break up over the phone, by text or by e-mail, but it may be the safest way. If it doesn't feel 100% safe, and if you don't feel comfortable doing it in person, then you *absolutely* have the right to break up without meeting in person.
>
> You do not owe it to a partner who has been abusive, or has ever threatened you, to meet in private to end the relationship.

If you feel 100% safe and choose to end the relationship in person, there is no need to be alone with this person in a private place. It should be done in a public place, and it would be wise to have a friend close by waiting for you to leave together.

You do not have to keep explaining your reasons for ending the relationship. It is your absolute right to end a relationship at any time you feel it is not right for you. It is every person's right to do so. You may say why you are breaking up, but your partner might twist all of those reasons and want to focus either on why they are not good reasons, or will promise to change those things.

It is important to remain firm and clear in your decision to end the relationship and to avoid getting into talking about "What if...?" A person who can be charming and persuasive might not be threatening at the time, but will likely try to "turn you around" on your decision and get you to give the relationship another chance, probably in a very emotional way. It can be emotionally difficult to end a relationship, but you decided to do it when you were thinking clearly. You probably came to the decision after thinking about it for a while, so it is appropriate to stick with your decision that you made while thinking clearly, rather than let your emotions change your mind again in the moment.

If an ex who has ever been physically violent or has threatened to be violent comes to your house or apartment trying to see you, friends should not open the door to let that person in. It is important to inform your friends, roommates, co-workers and manager at work that you are getting out of this relationship and that they should not accommodate for your ex trying to see you. It is completely fair to call the police if someone will not go away. If that sounds drastic, remember no one is supposed to live in fear of another person, and it is *this person's* actions that are bringing this about. An ex must learn to accept your wishes and your most basic rights of personal space. Some people might not realize how serious their actions are, and for some people, the authority of the police or the university is the only thing they will listen to.

If you, or any of your friends, feel afraid of your ex, there is probably a good reason. Do not talk yourself out of taking extra precautions. Talk with a professional on campus about your concerns so you can receive guidance and know your options.

It is usually healthy to break off contact with an ex, even from a relatively healthy relationship, but it is very important to break off contact with an ex from a bad relationship. After ending an abusive relationship, it is appropriate to break off contact, either for an extended period of time or forever. It is your right to do so, and it is better for both people.

The Right to be Free from Fear

You have the right to not be texted and called at all hours of the day and night by your ex. You have the right to not have your ex show up outside of your classes, your work or your home, or to do anything else that violates your wishes to end the relationship. It might be difficult to completely avoid running into your ex, especially if you are part of the same social group or are on a small campus, but your ex should not be actively engaging in pursuing you if you do not want that.

The words "harassment" and "stalking" might sound a bit strong when applied to this person you loved and still might care about, but certain behaviors do qualify as harassment or stalking. If you are not sure about whether or not your ex is actually crossing a line, then honor your concerns and talk with someone about it. Go to the counseling center, the Dean of Students, your Women's Center, or any trusted adult for advice on your options. Go with a friend and find someone who will help you learn about options and see the situation more clearly. Your school, workplace, or campus should have many great resources and be willing to help you and support you.

HELP IS AVAILABLE:
Call an abuse hotline (1-800-799-SAFE), chat live online at LoveIsRespect.org, speak with a professional on campus who is trained to understand abusive relationships, and do whatever is necessary to ensure your or your friend's safety.

If you do not feel your college or university is responding to help support your safety, contact your campus's Title IX coordinator. Also consider talking with college counseling services and local police. Both can be great resources and are familiar with stalking and harassment situations.

Moving Forward

You ended the relationship for good reasons, and there will come a time in your future when you are completely over it and are very glad you moved on. You already gave it many chances to work. It wasn't a healthy relationship, and you deserve a great, healthy relationship.

Focus on moving forward and becoming the best version of yourself. Focus on school. Focus on your friendships and your family. Focus on your own physical, mental, emotional and spiritual health. This is *your* life.

When to Say Something to a Friend

You are needed. Part of your role as a friend is to help those around you in a number of ways, not just in the most extreme and obvious emergency situations when almost any person would choose to help another, but in other times as well.

It is likely that, at some point in your life, a close friend will deal with an unhealthy relationship. Help create a culture of people who are able to help those around them.

When it comes to helping a friend who is in an unhealthy or abusive relationship, it is common for people to have thoughts such as:

> *At what point should I say something? Is my friend really in an "abusive" relationship, or is it just normal drama? I don't think he would physically abuse her. I don't know how to bring it up. It's her business anyway. I guess if it was really bad she would just get out of it.*

The time to say something is whenever you wonder if something is not respectful, healthy, and loving. It is always the right time to build up your friend's self-worth and belief that they deserve to be in a great relationship and to be treated with respect.

When looking for signs to determine whether or not your friend is in an unhealthy relationship, consider these factors:

- You've observed disrespectful behaviors yourself.
- They have told you about instances of mistreatment.
- You've heard stories about her/his partner's behavior that fit into the categories listed in the section on Warning Signs.

Other signs to watch for:
- Noticing that she seems to be afraid of her partner.
- Your friend tries to laugh off or joke about things their partner does that sound wrong to you.
- Your friend says they fight a lot, but tries to take the blame for it. Even if it might be true that your friend sometimes starts conflicts, verbal, physical, or emotional cruelty is never an acceptable response.
- Your friend seems to have changed, and is not as happy as she/he used to be.
- They seem to be controlled by their partner, even if they would not label it as that.

Tips for Supporting a Friend

People often wonder what to say to a friend in an unhealthy relationship because they don't want to offend them or make them defensive. It can be difficult to find the perfect words, but the good news is you don't need to be perfect. Just expressing that you care, are concerned, and are there to help is a powerful thing to do as a friend.

> **Avoid:** Try not to make broad critical statements about their partner like, "He's such a jerk. I don't know why you stay with him" or "She's so mean. I don't know why you're with her."
>
> **Do:** Keep the focus on your friend rather than on criticizing her partner. If you attack their partner, the natural response is for them to defend their partner and their choice to stay in the relationship. Even though they may have seen even worse behavior no one knows about, it is also true that they will have seen their partner's best qualities. It is those positive qualities that a person might think of if they feel their partner or their decisions are being "attacked."

It is also natural for a person to have feelings of embarrassment about being in a relationship with someone who has mistreated them, and they might actually fear the judgment of their friends. It can help to let your friend know that, though you are concerned, you do not judge her, and you understand the situation is complicated. Share what your concerns are about her happiness, and about anything you've observed that makes you have those concerns.

Avoid: Do not confront the other person directly, even if your friend has talked with you about specific abusive behaviors the other person has engaged in.

Do: Seek assistance. Supporting a friend in an unhealthy relationship can be stressful, and it can be difficult to know what to do. You do not have to do it alone. Talk with a counselor or other professional on campus for support and guidance. Go to loveisrespect.org to seek answers. From there you can also call or chat with an expert online for advice.

PERSONAL APPLICATION

Something that stuck out to me from The Strength of Moving on was _____

_____

_____

_____

Some reasons why a relationship wouldn't necessarily need to qualify as "abusive" in order for it to be time to end it are _____

_____

_____

_____

The tips from the authors of *When Dating Becomes Dangerous* that stuck out to me most were _____

_____

_____

_____

Suggestions from the Tips for Supporting a Friend section that made sense to me were _____

_____

_____

_____

_____

In a Relationship with Reality

The New Strategies for Social Safety

Whether you are driving a car in traffic or walking through a city, you naturally think about ways to increase your safety. By practicing those safer ways to drive or to walk through a city, you have a more enjoyable experience. It works the same way in the social world on campus, outside of school, or in your social life as an adult of any age. Although nothing absolutely guarantees safety, sticking to certain practices can increase the likelihood of having the great, safe social experiences that we all want, and helping your friends to do the same.

Reality-Based Safety
Beyond Dark Alleys and Scary-Looking People

In order to optimize your safety in high school, college, and beyond, and in order to help your friends and others be as safe as possible, it is important to have a clear picture of reality. The unfortunate truth is that most harm is not actually committed by psychotic strangers, but by "regular" people who simply think in a way that justifies taking advantage of their size or situation.

This means we must *expand* our basic safety precautions beyond typical practices such as avoiding the "bad" parts of town or not walking alone at night on campus. We must consider what precautions make sense in the social world around us, like at parties and social events when we are among friends and acquaintances. It is natural to want to assume we are safe when around fellow students, but the unfortunate reality is we just do not know whether or not this is true.

Below are some uncomfortable truths about the reality of the social world we live in, and unfortunately these truths are the same in every type of city, town, and campus. It is natural to assume seriously bad things happen "somewhere else." We have a tendency to think, "This place is different." But there is virtually no place where we can safely assume, "That would never happen *here.*"

REALITY:
Some people think it's fair game to try to get another person as intoxicated as possible, until that person is passed out or incapacitated, and then engage in acts with that person's body when they are "out of it" and incapable of resisting.

Reality:
Sometimes, an aggressor's peers do not realize how wrong and harmful it is to take advantage of a person who is incapacitated, and do not intervene or call them out on their behaviors. This results in them continuing to act in harmful ways.

Reality:
Some people do not care who they hurt, and it can be very difficult to tell who thinks this way. Sometimes those people are good at hiding who they are.

As mentioned at many points in this book, it is not fair that women have to constantly think about how to stay safe. We cannot, however, know who may have the potential to be dangerous, so certain safety precautions are essential practices in our lives. The following is not necessarily a complete list, but includes some of the basic safety precautions that are used by women (and men) on campuses and in cities throughout the country:

Agree in Advance

Make an agreement with friends ahead of time that you will keep track of one another and make sure everyone is safe before leaving a party, bar, or other social situation. Agree ahead of time with each other that if a person seems too intoxicated or is "out of it," she will need to go home with one of her friends, even if she would like to stay or go home with someone she met.

Fully Charged

Make sure your cell phone is fully charged before going out.

Out Together - Home Together

Stick to plans of going home with specific friends rather than by yourself.

Text Tomorrow

Utilize "Text me tomorrow," "Text him tomorrow," and "Text her tomorrow" when meeting new people, especially if you are removing a friend from a potentially unsafe situation. A person you meet at a party or at a bar can text you the next day if they are truly interested in getting to know you. Ending the night with friends, talking about things, and waking up in your own bed is safer, and it can also be a great way to end the night. It can also help to weed out anyone who is not serious about getting to know you as a person.

> *Caution:* The fact that a person texts you the next day or continues to show signs of interest after meeting for the first time does not automatically mean that person is 100% trustworthy. Trust takes time to be earned. It only makes sense that people should prove their trustworthiness over time.

Go With Them
If a friend has had too much to drink and needs to go home, it is not enough to put them in a cab or get them an Uber or Lyft. The thing to do is for one or more friends to go with that friend to make sure they get home and into bed safely. This includes making sure they are not at risk of alcohol poisoning, or of vomiting in their sleep and choking on their own vomit. If there is any doubt at all, it is important to call an ambulance for help.

In our social lives, it's easy to let down your guard so that a new person you meet can very quickly seem like a friend, and even a potential partner when, in reality, they were technically an adult stranger. We must consider the fact that even when we are surrounded by fellow students in a fun and friendly environment, we really do not know how each person thinks. Some people who seem to be non-threatening may have a mentality that would make them unsafe to others under certain circumstances.

It does not take a psychotic stranger to violate another person; all it takes is for a regular person to think in a way that would justify certain behaviors. Even otherwise decent people can rationalize their behavior and tell themselves something is "manly," "fair game" or "harmless" when, in reality, it is none of those things.

The Trust Principle

Principles help guide our thinking and decision-making. They are often better guides for us than feelings and opinions. My opinions, or your friend's opinions about a certain subject may or may not be helpful. Principles, however, are ways of understanding how things work. Principles help us know how to avoid more problems and experience more success.

Principles help clear up confusion.

THE TRUST PRINCIPLE:
It is not your obligation to trust another person right away. It is the other person's obligation to prove they deserve your trust. This takes time.

It is a positive character trait to look for the good in people, but seeing the good in a person does not mean trusting them. We base too much of our assessment of a person on their appearance and our initial interaction. If a person only needs to dress a certain way, smile, and be easy to talk with for a few minutes to gain your trust, then that is too low of a threshold for them to meet.

Here is what you can tell just by looking at someone: you can tell what that person looks like. That is about it.

Here is what you can tell about a person after talking with them for a while. You can tell what it is like to talk with them for a little while. That is about it. A first impression is only one impression—a first impression is an incomplete impression.

That is not how we really operate in a social world though, and that is why it is important to be aware of the tendency to put too much faith in our ability to discern another person's character just by looking at them or talking with them for a brief time.

You hear good things about a certain person, you can like talking with them, and you may have a great first impression of them, but none of those things means you should completely trust them yet.

A "good guy" is not offended by a woman not fully trusting him yet. In fact, a good guy actually wants her to have that mentality because he knows it is a good general attitude.

A "good guy" respects you for being aware that some guys are not worthy of trust, and he is glad you are careful to not trust people too much right away.

The Friend of a Friend Factor

In addition to a person's appearance and personality, we also place a lot of value on their associations and the activities in which they're involved. We too often give a person instant credibility because they are on an athletic team, in a certain fraternity, or part of a certain social group. If a person looks good, seems normal, and is a friend of a friend, most people see nothing but green lights with this person.

Trust should take time. It should not be won just by looks, personality, group affiliation, or even by being a friend of someone you know and respect.

Being a friend of a friend should not fast-track trust.

Most boys and men (and many women) have friends they know through school, sports, or work that they wouldn't necessarily assume to have perfect integrity.

You are not obligated to completely trust anyone, and certainly not until they've demonstrated a lot of reasons to suggest they are worthy of trust.

It's Not About How He Treats His Mom

When I am speaking to a group of students, sometimes I ask if anyone has ever heard the advice of considering how a guy treats his mother to see what kind of person he is. When I ask this, most hands go up.

I then ask if they have ever seen a movie in which a Mafia hit man is a brutal killer, has a mistress, but believes in treating his mother with respect. Most hands go up again.

It is not about how he treats his mom. Yes, a guy should treat his mom with respect, but that should not be seen as a great accomplishment.

What can you tell about a guy by how he treats his mom? You can tell how he seems to treat his mom. That is it.

It does not tell you how he would treat you in a relationship.

Most people have situational ethics, meaning they are good and decent in one situation but not necessarily in another. Most guys treat their friends, family, and dogs well, and even women well during their very first encounters and dates with them, but this treatment gives very little indication of what it would be like to be in a relationship with him.

PERSONAL APPLICATION

One thing from Reality-Based Safety that I think my friends and I should remember is _____

_____
_____
_____
_____

Something different, or especially important, that stuck out to me in the section on basic safety precautions in Reality-Based Safety was _____

_____
_____
_____
_____

The Trust Principle makes sense to me because _____

_____
_____
_____
_____

Understanding Alcohol & Sexual Assault

Alcohol is so closely associated with sexual assault that it is very important to understand how it is and is not related. Sometimes you might hear people say things like "Alcohol is involved in the majority of sexual assaults." It is important to clarify that alcohol is not responsible for sexual assault; the person who violates another person is responsible.

> *Alcohol is not responsible for sexual assault.*
> *The person who violates another's most basic rights*
> *is responsible for sexual assault.*

Three Realities Regarding Sexual Assault & Alcohol

1. **A Clear Conscience "Weapon" — A Tool Used to Increase Vulnerability**
   Alcohol can be used by those who do not care who they hurt as a way to make the other person incapacitated.

Alcohol is a much easier tool to use than a date rape drug, because it is seen by most people as a normal part of our culture.

Some who would never use a weapon or a date rape drug will think incapacitation due to alcohol is somehow different and that it is okay to take advantage of a person who is passed out or "out of it" from alcohol. Some people rationalize they are not doing anything wrong because in their mind they are different from what they imagine to be a "rapist."

Alcohol is a drug. The fact that it is a part of the American culture and college culture does not mean it should not be taken seriously. Even if alcohol consumption is a common part of a social environment, that does not mean drinking, or drinking too much, needs to be part of your experience.

2. The Critical Shift

One simple way of increasing safety practices for all people is simply to heighten our awareness of anyone who has had too much to drink. The most common way a person might be more vulnerable to harm of some kind on a college campus, or anywhere else, is being highly intoxicated or incapacitated from alcohol. Rather than focusing on trying to figure out who might be a dangerous person, it can be easier to just elevate your level of concern for *anyone* who is highly intoxicated.

The bad news is that it is pretty easy for a person to become highly intoxicated. The good news is we can often recognize when someone seems to have had too much to drink.

Our concern should be recognizing when a woman (or a man) is highly intoxicated. It is important, however, to focus not only on a person's level of intoxication, but also on anyone they might want to be alone with. A person who is highly intoxicated may disregard the basic boundaries and wishes of the other person when they are together in private.

If you find that a guy is highly intoxicated, encourage his friends to take care of him and make sure he gets home. A range of negative things could be avoided (even if nothing like a sexual violation would occur) by pointing out the situation to friends of a highly intoxicated person.

3. Being in Control Increases a Person's Ability to Remain Safe

Nothing absolutely guarantees safety. Some perpetrators commit their crimes when neither person is intoxicated. Instead, they use fear, intimidation, threats, their size advantage, or physical force to violate someone. Some use charm and social skills to gain a person's trust and attraction. Then they become coercive, highly pressuring, or use force to do what they want in a hookup situation. It is possible that a person who seems to be completely trustworthy will actually end up being dangerous.

Just as being in control and clear in our thinking increases our ability to do anything else, it also increases the likelihood of remaining safe. Remaining sharp can help you pick up on cues and signs of risk, whether for your own safety or for those around you.

Most people do not want to drink *too* much, but it can be difficult to gauge how much they can drink without it being "too much." Even older adults who are experienced drinkers often find it difficult to drink just the right amount that would not cause them to be "out of it" at some point in the night. When a person drinks mixed drinks, gets into a drinking game or does shots, it is even more difficult to moderate their level of drinking and know exactly how it will affect them that night.

KEY CONCEPT:
It is critical to always be clear that any person who violates another is the one responsible for the violating act —the person who harms another is responsible for his/her actions. But since we do not want anything negative to happen to anyone, we look for all possible ways to increase safety.

The Standard of Looking Out for Others

You are needed. Our culture needs you to use your caring eyes and ears to recognize when someone else might need help.

But looking out for others is not only about taking action in an emergency situation. The world changes and our culture evolves because of many small things people do. Most social change is led by young adults who recognize there is a better way of thinking, and they help educate those around them in simple ways.

Women have the power to influence those around them. When a woman comments on irresponsible attitudes and behaviors exhibited by her male friends, it makes a difference. Boys and men also have the power to influence people around them in a positive way. Women and men both make a difference when they help their friends understand why certain attitudes and behaviors are a bigger deal than others might realize.

Two Categories that Call for Intervention

Not An Emergency, But Important

Comments and attitudes revealed:
- Victim-blaming attitude
- Insensitive comment
- Sexist comments
- Mocking the importance of talking about serious issues as an organization
- Defending the actions of an abusive person
- Belittling or saying a demeaning or mean thing about a friend, or other individual

Ideas and plans that sound like they're not wise:
- Social plans that sound unsafe
- An activity that sounds like it could be emotionally difficult for some members

Potential Emergency, Or Emergency
- It appears someone is being hurt, physically or emotionally
- Someone could be seriously hurt, physically or emotionally

The Strength of Tact

> "Tact is the art of making a point without making an enemy."
>
> —Isaac Newton

A lot of people are not comfortable with confrontation, and even those who are comfortable with it often aren't good at it. It is natural to want to avoid causing drama. We are socialized to not make too big of a deal out of things, and I agree with that, unless something *is* or could be a big deal. With a little tact, you can avoid drama and say what you want to say, and make a point that could make a very big difference.

Tact is a critical skill to optimize your relationships with others as a professional in your career, as a friend, as a parent, and in personal relationships of all kinds. Being tactful can dramatically increase your effectiveness in dealing with people in any situation, and especially one that is sensitive or has the potential for conflict.

Tact allows us to be honest, while showing consideration for how the other person might feel about it. Tact is not about being submissive, it's about being assertive. Saying something tactfully is saying what needs to be said, but very carefully.

- Thinking before you speak and choosing words carefully.
- Approaching the issue as a friend, even if you don't know the other person.
- Avoiding unnecessary conflict, and allowing others to save face.

The Five Techniques of Tact

1. **Avoid starting sentences with the word "you" because it tends to make the other person defensive.**
   Many people are surprised to learn that even a *compliment* that starts with the word "you" can make people tense up and find it harder to accept your compliment. Starting a sentence with "you" sounds like a judgment, so even a positive judgment is less easy to accept than a compliment that starts with "I." For example, "I appreciate the way you guys have this whole party set up" is more impactful than "You did a good job setting up this party."

   When dealing with potential conflict, you may or may not be starting with a compliment, but the principle is the same that it is an effective communication practice to start sentences with "I" followed by a tactful phrase, rather than the word "you."

   Examples of "I" statements that can be helpful in a potential conflict situation include:

   - "I don't think you mean to say it quite like that."
   - "I think I understand what you're saying, and I know you don't mean to suggest _____, but…"
   - "I appreciate what you're trying to do. I just don't know if that's the best way to go about it. I'm thinking that…"
   - "I hear what you're saying. I don't know, however, if that's going to be the best way."
   - "Hey, what's up? I'm Aaron. I was wondering if you could help me out with something. Do you happen to know the guy over there with that girl who is out of it?"

2. **Use a "cushion" statement when you disagree with someone.**
   MindTools.com has a good article on "How to Be Tactful," referring to the statement before you respectfully disagree, or say something the other person might not want to hear, as a cushion statement.

   You might do this naturally with a friend or family member, possibly even saying multiple cushion statements before disagreeing or saying something they won't want to hear.

   To help you envision how cushion statements can be used, here are some examples with the cushion statement being in italics:

   - **EXAMPLE 1:** An example for when getting someone else to help out might be, "Hey, what's up – I'm Aaron. (cushion phrase) *I don't want to make too big of a deal out of something, but* (then share how it could be a big deal) it seems your friend is thinking of maybe taking that girl home and she's totally out of it, and that might be bad for everyone. She seems not capable of hooking up with anyone tonight, and I wouldn't want your friend to get in trouble or risk making someone really uncomfortable or accused of taking advantage of someone."

   - **EXAMPLE 2:** When wanting to add to a comment that suggests only women can experience "real" maltreatment in a relationship—*"I agree that* *abuse and maltreatment against women and girls is a HUGE problem.* I think it's also true that any person can be cruel and mistreat a partner, and that a boy or man can also be hurt from being verbally, emotionally, or physically mistreated by a partner.

- **EXAMPLE 3:** To her friends, or to other women – "Do you know that girl over there who seems out of it? *That guy who's talking to her might be a decent guy, but...* I definitely don't think she should go home with anyone tonight except her friends. Do you agree? I'm thinking someone needs to really keep an eye on her, maybe even take her home early.

- **EXAMPLE 4:** To a bartender, bouncer, or host of a party – "*Hey, I'm not trying to cause a problem, but* I feel like I need to point out that there's a girl over there who seems pretty out of it, and a couple guys I don't think she knows very well who seem like they're planning on taking her home. It just doesn't look good."

- **EXAMPLE 5:** When disagreeing with a comment in a conversation, such as someone defending a man's inappropriate behavior—"*I agree that these issues are complicated.* I also don't think it's an expression of strength for a man to use his size over someone smaller than him, especially in a relationship."

3. **"Sandwich" your point of disagreement between positives.**

   Sequence:

   1. Compliment/positive statement

   2. Point you want to make

   3. Positive statement that gives them the benefit of the doubt

   Constructive feedback, or correcting someone's outdated or ignorant perspective, can be placed in the middle of two positive statements.

   For example, "You're a smart guy. *I don't think it makes sense though that it's ever okay for a man to abuse his power over a woman.* But I'm sure you didn't mean for it to come across as justifying physical abuse."

4. **Say it with a smile.**
   Consider the body language of someone smiling a natural smile as they respectfully make a point, compared to a person walking toward you with his shoulders squared, looking you in the eye with a serious look on his face, and telling you that you're wrong or demanding you to do something. Which one would evoke defensiveness?

   It's more effective to approach someone as a friend, give them the benefit of the doubt that they also don't want anything negative to happen to anyone, and that they'll either get what you're saying or help you with the situation. Envisioning a confrontational approach is not only what keeps most people from doing or saying something, but it also can be much less effective than handling it in a tactful way.

5. **Tactfulness can also be blunt and to the point.**
In certain circumstances, being blunt and to the point in a simple statement can also be effective communication.

For example:

- "You don't mean that."
- "That's not right."
- "You don't want to do that."
- "You're crazy." (said with a smile and love, but definitely disagreeing)
- "I don't think that's a good idea."
- "I love you, but that's a bad idea."
- "Come with me. We gotta go."
- "Bad idea."

All of the above can be said to a friend or acquaintance in a way that is friendly, and clearly just wanting to help out.

Challenges & Solutions for Looking Out for Others

Challenge:
Worrying that confronting someone about their behavior will be a big deal and create a lot of conflict.

Solution:
Understanding that addressing a potential problem is a socially normal thing to do. Doing so is not really about conflict and confrontation; it's about helping *everyone* involved and *preventing* what could have been very serious.

Remember that if something negative could happen, then others really are on your side. *No one* wants something seriously bad to happen.

The friends of any person who might potentially harm someone else do not want that to happen. They likely care enough about human beings that they don't want their friend hurting someone, and even if they are especially immature and don't realize the harm it could cause, they have other motivations like not wanting their friend to get into serious trouble.

Remember that the person who is saying or doing something potentially harmful *probably* does not really want to harm anyone, and would probably be glad to wake up the next day and realize nothing bad happened.

Challenge:
You don't know what to say or how to say it.

Solution:
Keep it simple. Be respectful. Assume others will help.

Remember that giving a lecture or going off on a rant isn't the best way to communicate in any situation, especially when people are drinking alcohol, so you don't need to concern yourself with that approach. You can say a lot with just a few words.

Remember that you will rarely have to do it all on your own. Most situations allow you to have support from others immediately because they're noticing the same things, or would support you as soon as you have pointed out something doesn't look good. In many situations, there are people in charge of the party or group who would help you with any situation needing attention.

Remember to apply the Strength of Tact. Remember that being respectful and approaching another person in a friendly manner is both more effective and more comfortable than a more confrontational approach. The first attempt to influence another person should not be a combative or accusatory one, which would naturally put any person on the defensive. It might be necessary to take things to another level at some point, but it can be more comfortable for you and more *effective* to approach everyone with the mentality that you're on the same team.

It is reasonable to give others the benefit of the doubt. It is okay to assume, for example, that a guy trying to leave with someone who is overly intoxicated does not want the other person to have a disturbing experience, and he certainly does not want to be accused of being a perpetrator if that person would feel like that is what occurred.

Multiple Options:

There are a number of ways to do something to help a situation, and most of them do not need to involve you being confrontational or doing it all on your own.

Direct and simple – Explain the situation from your perspective:

> "She's out of it."
>
> "She's too drunk to hookup tonight or to go home with anyone. Text her tomorrow if you'd like to see her."
>
> "Let's find his friends and have them get him home."

Even though a person might be disappointed about not spending the rest of the night together, any decent person should respect the intentions of people just trying to make sure someone gets home safely.

Recruit others to help – Friends or those who have authority:

> Talk with your friends, their friends, or anyone you've been talking to that night who seems like a decent person.

If you're in a public place, accept that you and your friends don't have to deal with this on your own. Whether you are in a dorm, a bar, or even at a fraternity party, use those who have authority there to help you.

Everyone is trying to have fun at a party or at a bar, but those who are in charge of it do not want something negative to happen, and they should respect the requests of guests who are concerned about another guest and want to just make sure they get someone home safely.

PERSONAL APPLICATION

Since we cannot know who might think in a way that would justify taking advantage of a person who has had too much to drink, we are called to look out for anyone who might be vulnerable. Some of the things I could do to help a someone who seems to have had too much to drink are _____

_____
_____
_____
_____

In Challenges & Solutions for Looking Out for Others, some of the concepts in the Solutions sections that seem helpful to me were _____

_____
_____
_____
_____

Taking Action in Real-World Situations

There will likely come a time when you recognize there is at least the potential for something negative to happen. It is at those times when you are needed to do *something* that will make a difference in the situation.

The good news is that the best solution will often include getting *someone else* to help. In a potentially serious situation, getting other people's friends involved can be the most powerful way to make a difference. And if you ever feel like you need to say something to someone directly, the most effective approach is typically one in which you approach everyone as a friend, and make a very simple comment that helps to change the situation in a positive way.

The following are just a few examples of the possible scenarios you might encounter in which you could do something that might make a difference for another person.

Scenario:
It appears someone is trying to get a person who is already "out of it" to do more shots.

What could you do?
You could approach the person serving shots in a friendly way and say something like, "She's already messed up. I don't think you want to see her throw up all over the place."

You could talk with that person's friends (or find them) and, in a friendly way, point out that it seems to you that their friend is pretty drunk. Express that you're concerned, and help them realize, if necessary, they should keep their friend from drinking more and maybe get their friend home earlier than expected.

You could approach the vulnerable person and offer them a drink of water. Comment that they probably don't want to do any more shots because they'll want to feel okay tomorrow.

Scenario:
You notice a couple is arguing.

What could you do?
Decide you are going to keep an eye on the situation from a respectable distance. Alert a friend around you to the fact that a couple is arguing and you're concerned it will escalate in to something more serious.

Scenario:
You wonder if certain behavior qualifies as stalking or harassment.

What could you do?
Seek guidance online or on campus. If behavior makes you question whether or not it is harassment or stalking, then it is likely that something is not right. It is important to talk with a professional on campus about what your options are, and ask for guidance on how to handle it.

Scenario:
You see someone, or a group of people, start to take a potentially embarrassing picture or video of someone who is highly intoxicated.

What could you do?
Point out that it's not cool. Assertively tell them to put their phone away. Get their friends to help if necessary. Help the person directly by taking them to the restroom or other room. If a person's clothes are revealing something or they are exposed in some way, cover them up like you would if it were your best friend.

Make sure the person is responsive. Alcohol poisoning can kill, and we usually do not know how much a person has had to drink or how much would cause it. It is always wise to call an ambulance if you are in doubt.

PERSONAL APPLICATION

Some of the reasons it is very important to look out for any person who seems to have had too much to drink, or who is "out of it" for any reason are _____

_____

_____

_____

Considering the fact that we do not know who might think in a way that would make them potentially dangerous, some of the things I think we could do in our group of friends to expand safety precautions are _____

_____

_____

_____

It is important to remember that we are not only concerned about preventing harmful things from occurring, but also about speaking up to address hurtful comments because

_____

_____

_____

In a Relationship with Friends

Supporting a Friend Who Has Experienced Assault or Abuse

> Sexual assault and relationship abuse can be very difficult to understand. We need to equip all members of our society to know how to support a friend or acquaintance who shares that they have experienced abuse or assault of any kind.

Recognizing & Rising Above Victim-Blaming

Victim-blaming is when people blame the person who was harmed, rather than the person who did the harming.

The person who harms is responsible for the harm. The person who hits, shoves, or belittles is responsible for their actions.

Why Victim-Blaming is so Wrong:

- It can be very hurtful. It will add to the trauma of a person already harmed.

- It creates an environment that can make people afraid to report or afraid to share.

- It's inaccurate. It misplaces blame. Those who violate or abuse are responsible for violating or abusive actions.

Understanding the Behaviors of a Victim/Survivor

It is not fair to say how someone "should" act after an experience of being violated. Different people react in different ways to the same situation.

Almost any kind of reaction to a disturbing experience can be considered normal. One key error to avoid is assuming you know how a person who has experienced something very difficult should feel and behave. It is also incorrect to assume you can determine how serious the harm was by how a person is acting on any given day. People respond differently to traumatic experiences over time. The feelings a person has may vary from week-to-week, day-to-day or minute-to-minute.

You may have a preconceived notion about the behaviors and feelings a victim of sexual assault or abuse should exhibit. It is important to remember that even reactions that fall outside of those expectations can be normal responses to very difficult experiences.

For example, a victim/survivor of sexual assault could cry frequently or could be especially unemotional at times. Other behaviors could include being highly cautious and withdrawing socially, or partying in excess. They may avoid any sexual situation, or they may act promiscuously, even if they had not done so before the assault.

Not all survivors have clear images of the abuse or assault. Memories are stored differently during a traumatic emotional experience.

The point is you should never assume a person was not really sexually assaulted because their behavior does not match your expectations.

Things You Can Do to Support a Friend

If a friend shares that they were sexually assaulted or abused, it is natural to have concerns about your ability to help. While no amount of preparation may fully prepare you to feel confident in knowing how to support a friend, I hope each reader can feel like they have received a substantive education on things they can do, as well as some errors to avoid.

Six Ways to Support a Friend

1. It is okay to not know how to handle things. Simply respond as a caring friend and **listen** without judgment.

2. Offer to go with her for medical help, and to talk with a counselor or rape crisis advocate on campus. Support her in any way she may need.

3. Honest and simple statements like, "I'm glad you told me" or "Thank you for telling me" or "I believe you" can be very helpful.

4. Understand that you cannot understand. It is best to avoid saying you understand what another person is going through. It is better to be there for emotional support, to be a friend who listens and who encourages her to see this is not her fault.

5. Do not pressure them to report, and do not pressure them to *not* report. It is important for them to feel supported in their decisions, not pressured. A person whose wishes have been disregarded in a very disturbing way does not need anyone else neglecting to respect their wishes.

6. Encourage your friend to talk with a professional counselor if they are not already seeing one. And, if they are willing to do so but are not sure where to go, help them find a counselor. Your campus should have a well-trained, caring professional for them to speak with. The counselor should also know of additional resources on campus or near it that can be very helpful. If, however, the first people you speak to do not seem to be as helpful or sensitive as they should be, keep looking. Do not assume one unhelpful experience means counseling is not the right thing. Keep looking until you find one who understands sexual assault and is good at working with survivors of it.

For additional content and an online forum go to Pandora's Project at pandys.org.

Finding the Right Words

When we learn about a friend experiencing something very difficult, we want to say something but don't want to say the wrong thing. Below are some suggested things to say and to not say if you learn of a friend who is a victim/survivor of sexual assault.

What you could say:

"Thank you for telling me."

"I'm glad you told me."

"I hope you realize that wasn't your fault. It was the other person who wasn't supposed to act in any way that would cause another person harm."

"Any time you want to talk, I'm here for you."

"If you don't want to talk about it, that's okay. And anything you want to talk about, please know that I want to listen."

"I believe you."

"What can I do to help?" Offer to accompany your friend to the counseling session, or to talk with an official on campus or the authorities to report what occurred.

Some Things to Avoid:

Avoid asking questions that could be interpreted as skepticism. Survivors of sexual assault often fear they won't be believed, and almost any question can infer either judgment or skepticism, which can be very painful for a survivor who is confiding in a friend. It is helpful to reassure your friend that you believe her (or him).

Do *not* suggest that a victim/survivor should "just get over it" or "just forget about it." That kind of an approach might be an attempt to help and to be encouraging, but it is not helpful and can be very hurtful.

Do not share your friend's story with others without talking with them first and asking if they would like others to know. It might be that they don't want anyone else to know. It might be that they would like others to know and would prefer it is out in the open, but are too uncomfortable to envision sharing it themselves. If this is the case for a friend in a group of friends, or a sister in a sorority chapter, it could be a great help to her for you to be the one to share the information with others, *but* that should never be done unless it is her wish for you to do so.

If it seems evident that the person who assaulted them is a threat to the community and to others, you might consider talking with your friend more about reporting it to the university or to authorities, but it still must be their decision to do so.

Many survivors want to blame themselves, so it is important to make sure you do not feed that by suggesting they should have done something differently. (healthyplace.com)

Along with not suggesting what they should have done differently, *do not say what you would have done if you had been in the same situation.* That can be insulting and hurtful. The reality is you do not really know what you would have done in the exact same situation, with all of the same factors involved. Judging a victim/survivor's actions or thinking of what they should have done in *hindsight* is completely unfair.

PERSONAL APPLICATION

Something I want to remember from the Understanding the Behaviors of a Victim/Survivor section are _____

_____
_____
_____
_____

The things that stuck out most to me from the Six Concepts on Supporting a Friend were _____

_____
_____
_____
_____

References & Resources

Online Resources

loveisrespect.org
loveisrespect.org offers great information on abuse and assault that is written in plain language. Highly-trained peer advocates offer support, information and advocacy to young people who have questions or concerns about their dating relationships. They also provide information and support to concerned friends and family members, teachers, counselors, service providers and members of law enforcement. Free and confidential phone, live chat, and texting services are available 24 hours, 365 days per year.

Gottman.com
Dr. John Gottman is recognized internationally as an expert on relationships based on extensive research done on couples dealing with disagreements. The Gottman Institute provides multiple types of trainings, and Dr. Gottman's books are a good resource to consider.

WomensLaw.org
WomensLaw.org is a project of the National Network to End Domestic Violence. They provide legal information and support to victims of domestic violence and sexual assault.

pandys.org
Pandora's Project provides information, support and resources to survivors of rape and sexual abuse, as well as to their friends and family. They offer peer support to anyone who has been a victim/survivor of rape, sexual assault, or sexual abuse through their online support group, Pandora's Aquarium. They believe that connecting with other survivors is a valuable part of healing. Online support includes a message board, chat room, and blogs. It is free to join and is safely moderated by a diverse group of survivors.

healthyplace.com
HealthyPlace.com is the largest consumer mental health site, providing comprehensive information on a wide range of topics, including mental health concerns, psychological disorders, and psychiatric medications.

RAINN.org
RAINN stands for Rape, Abuse and Incest National Network. RAINN created and operates the National Sexual Assault Hotline (800.656.HOPE) in partnership with more than 1,100 local sexual assault service providers across the country.

If you or someone you know has been affected by sexual violence, it's not your fault. You are not alone. Help is available 24/7 through the National Sexual Assault Hotline at 1-800.656.HOPE, and online at online.rainn.org.

Online References

https://rainn.org/get-information/
sexual-assault-recovery/tips-for-after-an-attack

https://www.womenshealth.gov/publications/
our-publications/fact-sheet/sexual-assault.html

Books Referenced

Alberti, R., & Emmons, M. (2001). *Your perfect right: Assertiveness and equality in your life and relationships.* Atascadero, CA: Impact.

Bancroft, L. (2002). *Why does he do that?: Inside the minds of angry and controlling men.* New York, NY: Penguin.

Branden, N. (1994). *The six pillars of self-esteem.* New York, NY: Bantam.

Covey, S. (1989). *The 7 habits of highly effective people: Powerful lessons in personal change.* New York, NY: Simon & Schuster.

Evans, P. (2010). *The verbally abusive relationship: How to recognize it and how to respond.* Avon, MA: Adams Media.

Fairweather, L. (2012). *Stop signs: Recognizing, avoiding, and escaping abusive relationships.* Berkley, CA: Seal Press.

Kerner, I. (2005). Be honest, you're not that into him either: Raise your standards and reach for *the love you deserve*. New York, NY: HarperCollins.

McKay, M., Davis, M. & Fanning, P. (2009). *Messages: The communication skills book.* Oakland, CA: New Harbinger.

Murray, J. (2007). *But he never hit me: The devastating cost of non-physical abuse to girls and women.* New York, NY: iUniverse.

Occhiuzzo Giggans, P. & Levy, B. (2013). *When dating becomes dangerous: A parent's guide to preventing relationship abuse.* Center City, MN: Hazelden.

Parrot, A. (1988). *Coping with date rape and acquaintance rape.* New York, NY: Rosen Publishing.

Recommended Books

Be Honest—You're Not That Into Him Either: Raise Your Standards and Reach for the Love You Deserve, by Ian Kerner

But He Never Hit Me: The Devastating Cost of Non-Physical Abuse to Girls and Women, by Dr. Jill A Murray

Can I Kiss You?: A Thought-Provoking Look at Relationships, Intimacy, and Sexual Assault, by Mike Domitrz

Domestic Violence: What Every Pastor Needs to Know, by Al Miles

For Parents and Teenagers: Dissolving the Barrier Between You and Your Teen, by Dr. William Glasser

Healing the Shame that Binds You, by John Bradshaw

He's Just No Good for You: A Guide to Getting Out of a Destructive Relationship, by Beth Wilson

Honoring the Self: Self-Esteem and Personal Transformation, by Nathaniel Branden

How to Ruin Your Love Life, by Ben Stein

It's a Breakup Not a Breakdown, by Lisa Steadman

Lies at the Altar: The Truth about Great Marriages, by Dr. Robin L. Smith

Saving Beauty from The Beast: How to Protect Your Daughter from an Unhealthy Relationship, by Vicki Crompton and Ellen Zelda Kessner

Should I Stay or Should I Go?: A Guide to Knowing if Your Relationship Can—and Should—Be Saved, by Lundy Bancroft and JAC Patrissi

STOP SIGNS: Recognizing, Avoiding, and Escaping Abusive Relationships, by Lynn Fairweather

The Emotionally Destructive Relationship: Seeing It, Stopping It, Surviving It, by Leslie Vernick

The Gift of Fear: And Other Survival Signals that Protect Us from Violence, by Gavin De Becker

The Mask of Masculinity: How Men Can Embrace Vulnerability, Create Strong Relationships, and Live Their Fullest Lives, by Lewis Howes

The Seven Principles for Making Marriage Work, by Dr. John M. Gottman

The Seven Habits of Highly Effective Families, by Stephen Covey

The Six Pillars of Self-Esteem, by Nathaniel Branden

The Verbally Abusive Relationship: How to Recognize It and How to Respond, by Patricia Evans

When Dating Becomes Dangerous: A Parent's Guide to Preventing Relationship Abuse, by Patti Occhiuzzo Giggans and Barry Levy

Why Does He Do That?: Inside the Minds of Angry and Controlling Men, by Lundy Bancroft

About the Author

Aaron Boe is founder of Culture Strength, a consulting firm specializing in providing systems of training and curriculum to prevent sexual misconduct and mistreatment in relationships. Aaron and the CultureStrength brands are known for their innovative, Behavioral Ethics approach that influences behavior by elevating culture and equipping individuals for positive personal relationships of all kinds. Aaron is the developer of award-winning prevention programs. He speaks and provides trainings throughout the country for organizations, campuses, and schools. Aaron earned both his bachelor's degree and master's degree from Indiana University. He lives in central Indiana with his wife Lauren and their four children.

General
www.culturestrength.com

Athletics
www.completestrength.org

Acknowledgements

It is rare to be able to thank people publicly, and in print. I am seizing this opportunity, though I am certain I will leave out people who have been very important to me in my life.

To Mom and Dad. Because of who you are as people I have been able to live each of my days with the deep blessing of feeling loved by those whose love I needed most. These lines are taking me longer to write than some chapters because it is difficult to say enough in only a few words. Thank you for your patience, sacrifices, encouragement, and support.

And Mom—my favorite teacher—thank you for making the final version of this book much better with your edits and suggestions. As always, you cared enough to help in every way you could.

To Lisa. Between the two of us, you are the better one. You are the one who is full of goodness. I hope you have experienced enough positives from me in return. I have always known that more people in the world should be like you.

To Lauren. This book, and much of my work would not exist if it were not for your support and understanding. It takes me a long time to create something that is not just a big mess, and your patience and faith in me have been all anyone could ask for. Thank you.

To Kegan. You are full of decency and you will be a wonderful dad someday. I have loved every minute with you, and I am very happy for you to have a relationship full of love with Kim. You were obviously my greatest inspiration for *Letters to Kegan*, and I hope something within these pages can play a small part in your happiness.

To Natalie, Jack, Maggie, and James. I love each of you fiercely. You provide me with a burning desire to figure out ways to make this world better. You make it easy to write about how a person deserves to be treated. Each of you, and all other people, deserve to be appreciated and treated with basic respect.

For certain scholars and experts, it feels like it is not enough just to cite them in a list of references. Dr. Albert Bandura's work has elevated my understanding of the world, and his theories are infused throughout my work. Lundy Bancroft spent fifteen years counseling abusive men—work I am certain I could not do—to gain insights that I believe better equip us to prevent abuse. He then chose to do the work of compiling and sharing what he learned. Without those efforts we would all still be more in the dark on this critical issue. Dr. Jill Murray has done the saintly work of sitting with victims and survivors of abusive relationships as a therapist, and then shared her important message about non-physical abuse with the world. I will always remember the long flight when I made notes in the margins of *But He Never Hit Me*, and made an unconditional commitment to myself to do what I can to put critical knowledge into the hands of young people and the parents who love them.

I want to thank my editor, Katy Gehan, for her patience and intellect as she worked with me to bring this book to completion. Thank you, Jess Pettit, for taking the time to read every word and for making valuable suggestions. And I feel indebted to Abbe Erle for being a trusted advisor who helped with important choices in the final stages. This book will reach more people because of the contributions and guidance of Katy, Jess, and Abbe.

I'm quite sure that Amy Dismore Mehall must have suffered as she graciously read and edited my earliest, rough writings on these topics, and with my first book, *Letters to Kegan*. Tricia Forbes edited and contributed her intellect and support to advance earlier pieces of writing that now make up much of this book. Tricia is a better writer than I. Her comments made me a better writer, and I hope this book will encourage her to write several books of her own. Thank you, Dr. Brian Mistler, for your valuable suggestions on earlier drafts, and for your friendship. Chandra (Daffer) Essex, Sarah McCracken, and Will Frankenberger, as national staff and leadership of Delta Zeta Sorority, also read and made helpful comments to multiple earlier drafts of writing that now makes up significant portions of this book.

I will be forever grateful that I stumbled upon the Department of Religious Studies at Indiana University. What can you say about those who taught you to think on a deeper level? It was truly a world-class educational experience for me.

Thank you to my Southwestern family. The trajectory of my life changed significantly during that first summer work experience in college. Much of my work and the approach we at Culture Strength take would likely not exist without my experiences with the Southwestern Company, now called Southwestern Advantage. Thank you, Dan Moore, for your example and your encouragement. Thank you, Kaye Willis White, for recruiting me and teaching me to better understand people and how to communicate more effectively. Thank you for your example, wisdom, and friendship Joel Broadbent, Creig Soeder, Larry Salerno, and Michael Jones. Thank you, Barrett Ward—I learned a great deal from you Barrett. Thank you Tim Spidel, Mark Dunlap, Tim Sweeney, Anthony Maieron, and so many others for helping me build a stronger foundation and for your lasting friendship. I am grateful for every person I met through Southwestern with whom I've shared laughs and real conversations. You are bright spots in my life. Each of you helped me during difficult times. I am also thankful for each college student I was able to work with in the Southwestern summer work program, and the many friendships that remain.

To all my teachers and coaches, thank you for your time and energy. Thank you for showing up each day to both move me along the path and to show you cared.

I appreciate Mic Wilson, Ron Kraus, and Kappa Sigma Fraternity for the life-changing, positive experiences from being a Kappa Sigma that will forever be part of me.

I appreciate Zeta Tau Alpha's National Council for making the decision to seek prevention education, and for allowing me to partner with Zeta Tau Alpha to impact young women. I also want to thank the National Council and headquarters staff of Delta Zeta, Alpha Xi Delta, Sigma Kappa, Phi

Mu, Pi Beta Phi, and Kappa Delta Sororities. Thank you to the National Councils and staff of Sigma Nu Fraternity, Phi Gamma Delta, Alpha Tau Omega, Kappa Alpha Order, Phi Kappa Tau, Delta Sigma Phi, and Phi Kappa Psi for allowing me to partner with you to impact young people.

I am grateful to be associated with each of my colleagues at Culture Strength and Prevention Culture. Thank you, Andrew Campbell, Abbe Erle, Aaron Shelby, and Dr. Brian Mistler for helping advance what Culture Strength can do. We are just getting started.

For More Information

For more information about the types of services Culture Strength or Prevention Culture can provide for businesses, schools, campuses, or the U.S. military, or to inquire about a customized service, go to: www.preventionculture.com

Athletics directors, coaches, team owners, and league officials can contact us about customized curriculum and training for athletes and teams at: www.completestrength.org

Friendly Request

Thank you for reading *In a Relationship*. I hope it will help you in multiple ways over time, or help you help someone else you love.

If you feel it has been helpful to you or feel it could be valuable to another person, please take a minute to leave a review on Amazon. Leaving a review on Amazon could help others take a closer look and feel more comfortable trying it out for themselves or someone they care about.

Thank you very much.
Aaron Boe

Made in the USA
Columbia, SC
23 March 2019